eXtreme sports

eXtreme sports

THE ILLUSTRATED GUIDE TO
MAXIMUM
ADRENALIN
THRILLS

Joe Tomlinson

CARLTON

ISBN 1 84222 465 4

Printed in Italy

ABOUT THE AUTHOR

Joe Tomlinson is a business and marketing consultant based in Portsmouth, Rhode Island. He has been involved in extreme sports for several years. He created and wrote the original concept for NBC and Emap Publication's The Gravity Games, and was the extreme sports consultant to the producers of the closing ceremonies at the Atlanta Summer Olympics.
Joe enjoys snowboarding, boardsailing, surfing, sailing, motox, racing karts and an occasional bungee jump or SCAD dive. He lives in Portsmouth on the East Coast of America with his wife Amy and their five children; JJ, Elodie, Summer, Lucie and Jane.

Picture Acknowledgments
The publishers would like to thank the following sources for their kind permission to reproduce the pictures in this book:

Agence DPPI/F Clement; Allsport/Luciano Bosari, Shaun Botterill, Simon Bruty, Mike Cooper, Glenn Dubock, Tony Duffy, John Gichigi, Mike Hewitt, Bob Martin, Gary M Prior, Pascal Rondeau, Anton Want; Allsport/Vandystadt/Kurt Amsler, Pat Boulland, B Buffet, Marc Cazals, Gerard Ceccaldi, Sylvain Cazenave, Sylvie Chappax, Bernard Desestres, Vania Fine, Jean Paul Galtier, Didier Givois, Vincent Kalut, Stephane Kempenaire, Didier Klein, Bernard Lambolez, Jean Paul Lenfant, Jean-Marc Loubat, Richard Martin, Thierry Martinez, Alain Marty, Remy Michelin, Gerard Planchenault, Philip Plisson, Alain Revel, Francois Rickard, Pascal Tournaire, Simon Ward, Laurent Zabulon, Zoom; Allsport/USA/Nathan Bilow, Vince Cavatio, David Leah, Mike Powell, W. Sallaz, Tina Schmidt, Stephen Wade; Bluewater Freedivers/Terry Maas; Buzz Pictures/Tim Barnett; Buzz Pictures/Brent Bignell; Buzz Pictures/John Carter; Buzz Pictures/Steve Jackson; Buzz Pictures/Mike John; Buzz Pictures/Nick Hamilton; Buzz Pictures/Neale Haynes; Buzz Pictures/John Nash; Buzz Pictures/Sang Tan; Cannondale; Rick Doyle; ©Hobie Cat; James Hudson; Image Bank/Jon Love, Marc Romanelli, William Sallaz; Jason Lee; Brad McDonald; Phorum/Mark D Phillips; ©Schwinn 1994, Rex Features/Laski; Brian W. Robb; Stockfile/Steve Behr, Malcolm Fearon, Steve Thomas; Stock Newport/Bob Grieser, Daniel Forster; TSI/Adamski Peek.

Introduction

I have to assume that if you're reading this, you're interested in extreme sports. In fact, you may actually participate in one or more of the sports described within this book. It doesn't really matter though, because extreme sports are exciting, and that's why everyone wants to know what they're all about.

WHAT ARE EXTREME SPORTS ALL ABOUT? What is it that gets athletes charged up enough to put their lives at risk? Is it all just a big adrenaline fixation? I don't think so.

Which is not to say that there isn't a quest for an adrenaline charge in extreme sports—there is. Most athletes, however, who consider themselves to be extreme are not lunatics seeking an adrenaline buzz no matter what the consequences.

They get their adrenal rush because their skills allow them to perform safely under conditions that are dangerous or even life threatening. They can successfully do things that could kill those unfamiliar with their particular sports because they have dedicated themselves to performing within their limits, even while they have consistently challenged themselves to redefine what those limits are.

Extreme sports are about individuality, higher and higher levels of achievement, redefining performance boundaries, and the personal satisfaction that comes from trying your best. Extreme sports deliver a sense of accomplishment, whether you establish a new level of ability or simply challenge yourself while having a great time.

Extreme sports do not generally prohibit you from having fun because of your physical size or build, but they do require for you to be in shape. You can enjoy your sports without the threat of a 300-pound adversary slamming you to the ground or a competing 8-foot giant keeping you from your goal. What you are pitting yourself against in extreme sports, however, is a much less forgiving opponent, the Earth and its elements—Air, Land, and Water. To challenge "mother nature" is far more formidable than competing with any massive individual.

There is a level of respect that should be afforded all extreme athletes, whether they are experts or beginners. As the saying goes, "you have to be a kook sometime"— translation, you have to start somewhere. None of the extreme sports are easy enough for a first time attempt to be done well, or safely in some cases, without assistance or supervision. Extreme sports are passed down and across from athlete to athlete, and there is a true sense of satisfaction to be gained from introducing a newcomer to your extreme sport of choice.

The extreme sports movement has been quick to embrace the idea of the "crossover" athlete. Moving over from one extreme sport to another is encouraged. An expert snowboarder may find that mountain biking really turns them on, so they begin to develop their skills on a bike. That same snowboarder may also find that boardsailing is a thrill, and so begins the process of learning to boardsail. The snowboarding, mountain biking, boardsailing athlete may then decide to try kiteboarding, hang gliding, climbing, kayaking, or any other number of extreme sports. As they build their repertoire of sports, they become better

"crossover" athletes, and each extreme sport adds a little to their skills in other extreme sports by broadening their ideas on how things can be done.

How extreme sports have impacted on each other is really the story of the evolution of extreme sports until today. Some of the sports are very old, like bungee jumping. Some of the sports are more recent, like mountainboarding. Both have elements that can be found in other extreme sports.

The thrill of freefall was first bound in bungee, but it can be found in windsurfing, snowboarding, skiing, B.A.S.E jumping, etc. The joy of carving a turn on a mountain board is new, but it has its roots in surfing, skateboarding, wakeboarding, snowboarding, etc.

Extreme sports are about gravity, ingenuity, and technology. Gravity is the force that pulls climbers off rock faces, skiers down slopes and off cliffs, hang gliders toward the ground, and water downstream. Gravity makes warm air rise above cold, drives water to settle at the lowest available spot to create lakes and seas, creates the swirling mass of atmosphere that drives the winds. Gravity shaped our planet.

Ingenuity and technology are responsible for the multitude of ways we have discovered to use the forces of nature to enjoy nature. The evolution of extreme sports is a story of pushing available technologies and designs in order to improve performance. From high-tech fabrics to composite construction methods to innovations in design, extreme sports have evolved through the years thanks to the energies of many pioneers.

Extreme sports are exciting because they are full of energy and spirit. Of course, they are visually exciting, as the pictures throughout this book amply confirm. Most importantly, extreme sports have a life-affirming quality that stretches from the story of their evolution to the sheer pleasure they offer to those who participate at any level.

The world is a big place, with elements that offer plenty of challenges. Enjoy the planet and embrace the sports that celebrate being a part of it—extreme sports!

If you want to take your interest in any of these sports further, you should search the internet for activities and organizations in your area. Participate and have lots of fun!

Air
Sports

8

It's fair to say that sports performed in the air are extreme. It is also fair to say that taking part in these sports can be extremely life threatening.

FURTHER INFORMATION

BIBLIOGRAPHY
- *Bungee Jumping For Fun And Profit*, Nancy Frase, ICS Books, Inc., Merrillville, Indiana 1992
- *Skydiving*, Christopher Meeks, Capstone Press, Inc., Mankato, Minnesota, 1991
- *The Encyclopaedia of Dangerous Sports*, Missy Allen and Michel Peissel, Chelsea House Publishers, New York, Philadelphia, 1995

ASSOCIATIONS & CLUBS

B.A.S.E. JUMPING
- U.S. Base Association
  12619 Manor Dr.
  Hawthorne, CA 90250-4313
  Jean Boenish, Dir.
  Tel: (001) 213-678-0163

BALLOONING
- Balloon Federation of America
  PO Box 400
  Indianola, IA 50125
  J. Michael Wallace, Pres.
  Tel: (001) 515-961-8809
  Fax: (001) 515-961-3537
- Sport Balloon Society of the USA
  Menlo Oaks Balloon Field
  PO Box 2247
  Menlo Park, CA 94026-2247
  Peke Sonnichsen, CEO & Pres.
  Tel: (001) 415-326-7679
- Bill Harrop's "Original"
  Balloon Safaris cc.
  Email travela@aztec.co.za
  PO Box 67
  Randburg, 2125
  South Africa
  Tel: (0027) 011-705-3201/2
  Fax: (0027) 011-705-3203
- Dansk Ballonunion
  Kronhjorterg
  8270 Hojbjerg
  Denmark
  Contact: Henning Sorensen
- UK Hot Air Balloon Passenger Rides
  http://www.ftech.co.uk/balloons/index.hts
- *Balloon Life Magazine*
  2336 47th Ave SW
  Seattle, WA 98116-2331
  Tel: (001) 206-935-3649
  Fax: (001) 206-935-3326
  E-mail: tom@balloonlife.com
- Aerostar Balloons (retailer)
  http://www.aerostar.com/

BUNGEE JUMPING
- North American Bungee Association
  Casey Dale
  PO Box 121
  Fairview, Oregon
  97024
  E-mail: NABA@bungee.com
- UK Bungee Club
  http://www.adren-a-line.com/bungeeindex.htm
  226 Baker Street
  Enfield, Middlesex, EN1 3JY
  Tel: (0044) (0)208-366-1766
  Fax: (0044) (0)208-366-5733
- List of Worldwide Bungee Jumping Sites
  www.bungee-experience.com/list.htm

HANG GLIDING
- U.S. Hang Gliding Association
  559 E. Pikes Peaks, Ste. 101
  PO Box 8300
  Colorado Springs, CO 80933-8300
  Jerry Bruning, Exec. Dir.
  Tel: (001) 719-632-8300
  Fax: (001) 719-632-6417
- British Hang Gliding and Paragliding Association
  www.bhpa.co.uk
  The Old Schoolroom
  Loughborough Rd.
  Leicester, LE4 5PJ
  Tel: (0044) (0)116-261-1322
  Fax: (0044) (0)116-261-1323
- Hang Gliding Federation of Australia
  PO Box 558
  Tumut NSW 2720
  Tel: (0061) 069-47-2888
  Fax: (0061) 069-47-4328

IMAGINE THE CONSEQUENCES of a parachute that doesn't deploy or deploys only half way, a balloon that suddenly deflates, a glider caught in a violent downdraft, or a sky surfer spinning out of control. Air offers little resistance, so it can't keep the forces of gravity from drawing our bodies to the earth's surface. Only the drag created as objects pass through the air limits the speeds at which they travel down to earth. Another useful fact about the air that covers our planet is that it varies in temperature. Warm air rises until it cools in the upper atmosphere, and then it travels downward once again to the earth's surface. Here, it is warmed again, and the cycle is complete. The air is much like an ocean, with its ever flowing tides and currents. Because the elements that make up the air are lighter than the ocean and the land, the air knows no borders. When it pushes up against land or sea, it simply follows the path of least resistance and moves on to pursue its intended direction. Understanding how air travels as it crosses the planet is of paramount importance to the creation and growth of extreme air sports.

TO FLY LIKE A BIRD

We have discovered a number of ways to defy gravity in the air. First we used vines and cords. Then we made balloons, parachutes, and wings, and using these to channel the air to create lift or sufficient drag to control the speed at which we fall to earth, we created sports that our ancestors could only dream about. Legendary Icarus was said to be the first to test the limits of flight only to perish in his famous tumble to earth after flying too close to the sun. Leonardo Da Vinci drafted many sketches after envisioning craft capable of flight, from the balloon to the helicopter. A

few short decades ago, many of the techniques currently used to test the air could have only been imagined in the pages of Flash Gordon or a Jules Verne novel .

The thrill of flying like a bird, hurtling to earth at high speed only to float to a stop, is what has drawn athletes to push the limits of what is possible in the air. One can only imagine that early balloonists would have considered it insanity if anyone had suggested jumping from their craft attached to an elastic cord or a parachute. Of course, these pioneers of aviation were then considered to be the crazy risk takers for pursuing flight. They were the early extreme air sports enthusiasts. In time, they were forced to create vehicles, namely parachutes, that could allow them to escape their balloons with their lives if the worst were to occur. Soon items of necessity became ones of play, and the limits of air were again redefined.

DEFINING THE POSSIBLE

Now athletes are surfing, flipping, gliding, and bouncing through the air in defiance of gravity. The opportunity to jump from aircraft is less than a century old. The first bungee jumpers used vines to break their fall to earth. There was a day when a high wire walk was a circus trick. It is safe to assume that during the course of the next century, athletes will continue to redefine what can and can't be done in the air until what is cutting edge today becomes commonplace.

Right now we can feel satisfied that all of the currently defined limits are newly defined. In the years ahead new boundaries will be established and what is in these pages may become arcane. Either way, there is no question that the core emotion and andrenaline rush that comes from pushing the limits of what can be done in the air will remain, and athletes will continue probing and testing the boundaries of aerial extreme sports.

■ Nervures (France)
Z.I. Point Sud
F-65260 Solom
France
Tel: (0033) 562-922-018
Fax: (0033) 562-922-025

SKI JUMPING
■ Duluth Ski Club
Duluth, MN
contact Jim Denny (001) 218-724-0092
■ Minneapolis Ski Club
Mpls, Mn
(001) 612-943-8956
■ Ontario Nordic Ski Club
Thunderbay, ON, Canada
Contact: John Lockyer
(001) 807-768-8575
■ St. Paul Ski Club
St. Paul, MN
Contact: Arnie Miller (001) 612-770-1650

SKY DIVING
■ U.S. Parachute Association
1440 Duke St.
Alexandria, VA 22314
E-mail: uspa@uspa.org
Tel (001) 703-836-3495
Fax (001) 703-836-2843
■ Canadian Sport Parachuting Association
4185 Dunning Road
Navan, ON K4B IJ1
Canada
Tel/Fax: (001) 613-835-3731
■ Parachute Association of Ireland
Moyne Lodge
Moyne Road
Buldoyle
Dublin 13
Ireland
Tel: (00353) 01-832-0802
Fax: (00353) 01-864-1170
■ Skydiving Magazine
1725 N Lexington Av
Deland FL 32724
E-mail: editor@skydivingmagazine.com
■ Parachutist (magazine)
1440 Duke St.
Alexandria
VA 22314

SOARING
■ Soaring Society of America
PO Box 2100
Hobbs, NM 88241-2100
Larry P. Sanderson, Exec. Dir.
Tel (001) 505 392 1177
■ Collegiate Soaring Association
4671 Kipling Street
Wheat Ridge CO
80033-2855
John H. Campbell
Tel (001) 303-860-0484
Fax (001) 303-556-6257
■ Soaring Society of South Africa
www.sssa.org/sssa_whatis.htm
Tel: (0027) 11-894-4377
■ Soaring Society of Canada
wwwsac.com
Suite 107
1025 Richmond Road
Ottawa, Ontario
K2B 867
Tel: (001) 613-829-0536
Fax: (001) 613-829-9497
■ Federation Française de Vol á Volie
www.ffvv.org/index.htm
29, Rue de Sèvres
75006
Paris
France
Tel: (0033) 01 4544-0478
Fax: (0033) 01 4544-7093

11

B.A.S.E. Jumping

If any of the extreme sports can be considered truly high risk, then B.A.S.E. Jumping is that sport. For those readers who are unfamiliar with the term "B.A.S.E.", it is an acronym for Buildings, Antenna Tower, Span, Earth. B.A.S.E. jumpers are athletes who leap from objects which fall under the categories B.A.S.E. represents. Generally these objects are not very high off the ground, and so the jumper must deploy his parachute very quickly or risk impacting the ground at deadly speed.

ACCORDING TO *The Skydiver's Handbook*, evidence exists that suggests B.A.S.E. jumping can be traced back as far as 900 years. Whether or not these jumpers survived to leap again is unknown. Modern B.A.S.E. jumping is believed to have started in 1978, where daring parachutists first began jumping off of El Capitan, a 3,000 foot (915m) cliff high above Yosemite National Park. This site has remained a hotbed for U.S. B.A.S.E. jumpers.

The term B.A.S.E. was coined by B.A.S.E. pioneers Phil Smith and Jean Boenish. By January of 1981, the first four B.A.S.E. jumpers had completed jumps in all four B.A.S.E. categories, giving birth to the U.S. B.A.S.E. Association. As jumpers successfully complete all four categories, they receive their official B.A.S.E. number. Phil Smith of Houston, Texas is B.A.S.E. #1.

B.A.S.E. has an outlaw reputation in the U.S., and is illegal. There are several countries worldwide where B.A.S.E. is legal. Some of the more well known legal sites are in France, Norway, and Brazil.

One of the most daring and highly publicized illegal jumps in the U.S. was made by John Vincent of New Orleans, Louisiana. John climbed to the top of the Saint Louis Arch using suction cups as handholds, and jumped. John was later arrested by the FBI for jumping from a national monument, and spent 90 days in a federal prison.

Jumps in the U.S. are now punishable by up to one year in jail and $5,000 (£7,500) fine.

Redeployment point

Anyone considering becoming a B.A.S.E. jumper or doing any type of B.A.S.E. jump should have completed at least 100 skydives. B.A.S.E. jumpers must be extremely familiar and comfortable with their gear. The jumper must have particularly strong freefall skills, as the ability to maintain correct body attitude during freefall is key to a safe deployment and landing. The need for excellent canopy skills should not be underestimated. Obviously, a jumper whose chute doesn't open properly or immediately, must possess the skills necessary to open or

Sometimes illegal and always dangerous, B.A.S.E. jumping is a truly high-risk extreme sport.

Putting things in perspective. The appeal of B.A.S.E. jumping is not obvious to everyone, but this jumper's intentions are clear.

redeploy the chute immediately, or that jump could well be their last.

The fundamental equipment used in B.A.S.E. jumping is the same as that used in parachuting. However, because B.A.S.E. jumping requires a much faster deployment, some of the traditional equipment must be modified. An example is the pilot chute, which is used to deploy the main parachute. Pilot chutes are always deployed by hand in a B.A.S.E. jump. Depending on the distance of the freefall, the jumper may elect to hold the pilot chute in their hand or stow it in an easily accessible pocket on their pack. The jumper may also elect to use a small or large pilot chute depending on how quickly the

main chute must be deployed. Some freefalls can be as small as 250 feet (76m), with only a few seconds separating the jump and any potential impact. Jumpers tend to use the hand deployment technique in short freefalls to reduce the potential for a missed pilot chute deployment and the resultant impact. Freefalls of 3,000 feet (915m), such as Angel Falls in Venezuela, can generally be done with the pilot chute stowed for deployment.

No time to think

Different jumps require different types of main parachutes, otherwise referred to as the "canopy." The selection of the correct canopy is critical to insuring a consistent and timely

deployment. Most B.A.S.E. jumpers prefer wing-like "ram air" canopies. Ram air chutes deploy very rapidly and afford the jumper more control and steering precision than the traditional round canopies. Quick deployment and steerability are particularly important when jumping from objects like antennas, which are secured by high-tension wires, or cliffs, which may have sizeable outcroppings which must be avoided. Ram air canopies provide the jumper with a directional deployment, whereby the jumper can be sure of continuing their predeployed direction on deployment. Additionally useful is the ability to steer the canopy away from objects on the ground, such as a river...or waiting police. Therefore it is easy to understand how jumping off the Empire State Building can pose an entirely different set of challenges than jumping from a 1,000 foot (300m) waterfall.

Part of the ritual of B.A.S.E. jumping is the climb to the "exit point." The process of climbing to the exit point is as much a part of B.A.S.E. jumping as the jump itself. It is during the ascent to the exit point that the jumper must carefully consider all of the aspects of the jump they are about to make. Visualizing the jump before it takes place during the climb allows the jumper to establish a mental image of what they are about to do, step by step. This is especially important since there simply is not enough time to think about it on the way down.

Each B.A.S.E. jump is unique. The jumper must consider all aspects of the jump prior to making it, or risk discovering an overlooked item during freefall. Only by fully considering each fall can the jumper make the most critical decision in every B.A.S.E. jump—whether or not to jump.

The ability to differentiate between a jump that can be made, and one that can but shouldn't, is probably the most important skill any B.A.S.E. jumper can possess. This is the ability to preserve one's existence based on a calculated judgment, not a simple roll of the dice, and this is what makes B.A.S.E. a sport.

Even though B.A.S.E. jumpers are extremely safety conscious, there is still a statistically high incidence of fatality. In the U.S. during the past two decades, over 20 people have died while B.A.S.E. jumping. These numbers only reflect those who have been killed, the number of those severely injured by non-deployment or partial deployment may be substantially higher.

I once met a B.A.S.E. jumper named Rick Harrison while with Phil Smith. Rick jumped from a building, had a partial deployment, and crushed both legs on impact. He proudly showed off his scars, and still jumps today. Given the meteoric rise in the popularity of B.A.S.E. jumping, it is fair to assume that the numbers of fatalities and injuries will increase.

For those of you who feel that B.A.S.E. jumping may be for you, be sure to find an experienced B.A.S.E. jumper or organization in your area before attempting any jumping. It is not the opinion of the author that B.A.S.E. jumping is safe, and only those with the required experience, and who are exercising good and sober judgment, can decide if they should attempt B.A.S.E. jumping at all. For those that do, I wish you good luck.

(Left) B.A.S.E #1 Phil Smith does the unthinkable, leaping off a speeding train crossing a span in pursuit of his #1 sport.

(Below) This antenna tower jump requires all the skills of the world's top B.A.S.E. jumpers.

Ballooning

Floating about the clouds without a care is a feeling that many would like to be able to enjoy. In fact, of all the extreme sports, this may be the one that has the most universal appeal, in its less extreme forms of course. By that I mean ballooning for relaxation, and not the limit-testing stuff like altitude record setting or distance record setting. Recreational Ballooning is an easy sport to try out, as most regions of the world have commercial operations of some sort.

WHAT HAS BEEN REFERRED to as "The Holy Grail" of ballooning is the around the world attempt. As yet never successfully accomplished, the logistics required are enough to end most attempts, if the weather doesn't. Only a brief weather window exists each year when a trans-global balloon trip is even remotely possible, between mid-November and mid-February. During this time, global jetstreams capable of driving a balloon fast enough to make an attempt feasible are typical, but

A burner heats the air trapped within the balloon, creating lift. The pilot adjusts the lift generated by controlling the air's temperature – warmer to rise, cooler to sink.

often erratic. As recently as late 1995 trans-global attempts have been readied, most notably by Richard Branson of the Virgin Group. His attempt in a massive 900,000 cu ft (2,743 cu m) balloon proved that no amount of money or preparation can make the weather co-operate. Of the two other attempts that year, only one got off the ground, and that only briefly. Trans-Atlantic and trans-Pacific flights are more likely to succeed, and have several times. The most difficult and lengthy is the trans-Pacific.

Not anyone can fly a balloon, it requires a license. However, the examination process is not nearly as difficult as what is required of an airplane pilot—generally ten hours of lessons and one hour of soloing. A written test is required in most countries, consisting of ballooning rules and meteorology knowledge.

Almost all modern recreational balloons use air heated by a propane burner shot into the bag (or envelope) to create buoyancy. The burner is used constantly to keep the air inside the envelope warm enough that it maintains or gains altitude, as it is constantly cooled by the surrounding air temperatures. To descend, the pilot allows the air within the envelope to cool enough that the balloon loses altitude. If a rapid descent is necessary, a vent on top of the envelope is opened.

A basket, or gondola, is attached to carry passengers. Balloons are not steerable, so the pilot is at the mercy of the wind. Therefore, each balloon flight requires a ground crew who can follow the craft and meet it on landing. Flights in wind speeds exceeding 10 mph (16kph) are not recommended, and altitudes of 2,000 feet (600m) are roughly all that is sought unless there are mountains to cross. Top pilots can steer the balloon if they are aware of the wind direction at each altitude level. Since the wind directions vary with altitude, a good pilot can raise and lower their balloon to get close to where they want to go.

Ballooning is one of the oldest extreme pursuits in recorded history. Flight using a

Relaxation, ballooning style, over the Tunisian desert.

balloon was first successfully accomplished in late August of 1783—a busy year—when the Charles Balloon was launched at Champ de Mars, France by Ann-Jean and MN Robert. One month later, Etienne Montgolfier successfully launched the first passenger-carrying balloon under a waterproof envelope made of linen. The "passengers" were a sheep, a rooster, and a duck. Only the sheep was at risk.

First air accident

Next, Montgolfier joined with army officer Pilâtre de Rozier to build the first manned hot air balloon. On October 15, de Rozier rode the balloon up to 84 feet (26m), and stayed there for approximately 25 minutes. He reported after landing that there was "nothing up there to worry about," however he was said to be quite pale when making the statement.

De Rozier soon made an appeal to King Louis XVI to sponsor a manned hot air balloon flight, "for the honor of France." Benjamin Franklin was in France during 1783 and reported the balloon's weight to be 1,578 lbs (716.4kg), with a lifting force of 578 lbs (262.4kg). So began the race to define the possible in ballooning. In December Jacques Alexander César Charles invented and launched the first hydrogen balloon—the first

to possess a valve designed to release gas for quick descents. He also used sandbags to provide discardable ballast, and a barometer to measure altitude.

Opera singer Madame Thible broke the gender barrier by becoming the first female aeronaut during a flight from Lyon in June, 1784. The first recorded flight across a body of water was made by America's first aeronaut, Dr John Jeffries, a Boston medical student. Jeffries, with Jean-Pierre Blanchard, crossed the English Channel in January, 1785. Another limit of manned flight tested and broken. A less happy event took place in the same year, when pioneer aeronaut de Rozier became the first victim of an air crash. His revolutionary combined hot air and hydrogen-filled balloon burst into flames, and he fell to his death.

Strategists quickly noted that using a balloon allowed for a complete view of the opponents' layout and fortifications. In April of 1794, the first military ballooning school was began in Meudon, France. Luckily, ballooning's strategic importance was short lived with the appearance of the airplane, and so balloonists were once again left to their own devices where they could dream of testing the limits of balloon flight.

Ballooning festival in Metz,
France, home of the Montgolfières.

Bungee Jumping

The moment of truth: when the excitement overrides any physical discomfort.

The idea of experiencing a free fall only to be snatched from the jaws of death by a cord attached to the ankles is not new. Modern bungee jumpers can trace the roots of their sport back to an ancient legend told by the native tribe of Pentecost Island in the South Pacific.

VARIOUS VERSIONS of the legend exist, but the basic plot surrounds a woman who was fleeing an abusive husband. The woman climbed a tall tree and tied a vine to her ankles. Her husband followed her up and when he lunged to grab her she jumped out of the tree. He fell after her, dropping to his death while his wife was saved by the vine. Depending on who tells the story, the men of the island started to repeat her stunt either because they were impressed by her show of courage, or just in case their wives tried the same trick. Needless to say, only men are permitted to participate in these ceremonies.

The practice soon evolved into a harvest ritual. Each year the natives build a jumping tower on the side of a hill, clear all the rocks and sticks away, and pulverize the dirt to soften the impact of landing. The ritual was first seen by western man when a couple of *National Geographic* writers visited the island in 1955 and reported on the practice of "land diving." It wasn't until 1970 that another *National Geographic* reporter named Kal Muller became "the first outsider known to attempt the heart-stopping plunge."

"With incredible precision (the cord) snapped taught," reported Muller. "My head barely touched dirt as I rebounded, finally coming to rest upside down...I felt oddly unshaken. The excitement had overridden any physical discomfort."

Muller's jump led to other stories about the ritual and in 1979 Oxford University's Dangerous Sportsman's Club got a hold of the idea and jumped from the 245-foot (75m) Clifton Suspension Bridge in Bristol, England. Then they brought the idea across the Atlantic, jumping from the Golden Gate Bridge in San Francisco and from a bridge spanning Colorado's Royal Gorge. With that the bungee movement in the U.S. was born.

The early U.S. bungee jumpers were based mainly in California and spent a lot of time jumping off bridges in the Sierras. In 1987 New Zealander AJ Hackett brought a lot of attention to the sport with a jump off of the Eiffel Tower. Also in 1987 the first commercial operations were started by Hackett in New Zealand and Peter and John Kockleman in the U.S.., each using very different systems.

Two systems

The New Zealand System uses a single, all-rubber cord that is shortened or lengthened depending on the weight of the jumper. A towel is wrapped around the ankles and the cord is attached with nylon mesh webbing. At Hackett's commercial operation, the jumper is also attached to a static safety line.

The U.S. system utilizes military-spec nylon-wrapped shock cord and the connection is made with rock climbing harnesses and locking carabiners. Instead of lengthening or shortening the cord to accommodate weight, U.S. jumpers add or subtract shock cords. The basic formula is one cord for each 50 lbs (23kg), and each cord has a static breaking strength of 1,500 lbs (680kg), making each cord the weakest link in the system. U.S. jumpers also use two harnesses (either waist and shoulder, or custom ankle) and two anchor points for added security.

Each system has its own feel. The U.S. system is more expensive and technical. Its 2:1 stretch ratio means more free fall and greater deceleration as the cord "catches" and begins to slow the fall. The New Zealand system has a 4:1 stretch ratio, which means that the cord is shorter and catches sooner, especially for heavier jumpers, an arrangement that is generally regarded as more comfortable.

In both systems, the energy from the jump is stored in the cords while they stretch until the fall is stopped. The stored energy then propels the jumper back upward for an additional sensation and a few subsequent free falls before the jumper comes to rest.

...to the bottom.

Bungee jumping is considered one of the most dangerous extreme sports. In fact, it may be the safest. Whatever your point of view, a bungee jump is pure adrenaline, from the top...

Bungee jumpers soon tired of simple jumps from structures and bridges and started jumping backward, by hanging from their hands or feet, or holding various positions. Others began adding novelty to bungee by jumping off in kayaks, garbage cans, riding unicycles, and other somewhat silly things.

Jumping together

Hardcore bungee jumpers soon began "sandbagging" to increase the intensity and height of rebound they received from the cords. Jumpers sandbag by holding onto added weight until they reach the bottommost point of the fall, where they release the weight. This method allows a 150 lb (68kg) jumper to be propelled upward with the stored energy of a 200 lb (91kg) jumper by releasing 50 lbs (23kg) at the bottom of the fall.

Springing back this way resulted in a whole new set of problems, since it was now possible to be propelled higher than the point from which the jumper sprang. Jumpers took care of this by using a pendulum approach that ensured they are propelled up and away from their point of take-off. With the pendulum system, the cords are secured on the opposite side of the bridge from the jumping side. This causes the jumper to arch down into the free fall and arch up and away from the bridge on the other side.

24

The new extremes of bungee jumping include leaping from helicopters and balloons, in a quest to add to the distance of the free fall.

As if sandbagging wasn't dangerous enough, jumpers soon began sandbagging using other jumpers as weight. The result of "the human sandbag" was a rebound that could send the jumper well above the launch point. More than a couple jumpers have been killed or seriously injured when their partners let go too early (sometimes hundreds of feet from the ground) due to the severe forces from the initial deceleration. Others have been lucky enough to survive falls as high as 150 feet (45m).

Jumpers have plunged from balloons and helicopters, seeking to add to the distance of the free fall. A handful of bungee jumpers are said to have free-fallen in excess of 1,500 feet (457m).

In an effort to increase the level of skill required to bungee jump, new competitive approaches to bungee are being tested. Competitions that require accuracy by grasping specific targets on the ground or in the water have added a new and exciting dimension to the sport. Other more acrobatic requirements are also being integrated into bungee.

Bungee is very safe for beginners. Bungee is often considered one of the most dangerous extreme sports, when in fact it may be the safest. There have been reports of injuries to jumpers' limbs and eyes from the shock of the deceleration, however, such reports have been grossly exaggerated. In fact, statistically, it is far safer to bungee than to drive a car, and of those who have been killed or injured while bungee jumping, all events were the result of human error.

As long as the jumpers have a complete understanding of the stretch of the cords, the distance of the fall, and the weight of the jumper, the jump should be uneventful. The fact is that if all of the safety considerations are met, the cord will stop the fall just as well as brakes stop a car when traveling downhill at speed to a stop sign on a cliff.

This jumper adds to the
thrill by going backwards.

Hang gliding is unquestionably the closest a human being can get to flying like a bird. Hang gliding is the essence of non-motorized, unassisted flight many of us have all dreamed of from time to time.

THE SPORT OF HANG GLIDING continues to progress today, as new technology allows the use of lighter and stronger materials. Extreme hang gliding is found only at the top expert level, where pilots can do virtually every trick imaginable, from full barrel rolls to inverted maneuvers. Stunt flying is a rapidly growing, and dangerous facet of hang gliding.

Records in hang gliding deal with extreme distance and altitude. Distances of more than 200 miles (320km) and altitudes above 10,000 feet (3,000m) are not uncommon. Larry Tudor currently holds the records for both distance and altitude. In 1985, Larry set the height record of 14,250.69 feet (4,343.61m) above Horseshoe Meadows, California. In 1990, Larry set the distance record of 303.35 miles (488.1km) in Hobbs, New Mexico, a longtime favorite spot for hang gliding.

Leonardo Da Vinci too dreamt of flight, and drew many flying machines during his life. A few are remarkably similar to today's hang gliders. The first manned hang glider flown was designed built and flown by German inventor Otto Lilienthal in 1893.

Hang Gliding

The closest a human being can get to flying like a bird.

The Wright brothers are said to owe much of their success at piloting their first motorized flight to their experience piloting hang gliders. However, with the emergence of power aircraft, hang gliding all but faded away into obscurity.

Looking for thermals

In the early 1960s, NASA began searching for a way to safely return the Gemini two-man orbital spacecraft to Earth. Scientists Francis and Gertrude Rogallo, in answer to NASA's request, invented a flexible wing that would allow the spacecraft to maneuver and land without the need for a parachute. This triangular wing design, known as the Rogallo Wing, is what lead to the design of the first sport hang gliders. The Rogallo design created a foil that was far easier to fly and control, and thereby opened the sport of hang gliding up to a whole new group of enthusiasts.

Pilots launch their hang gliders from hills or cliffs from a running start to generate the initial lift necessary for flight. Once airborne, the pilot must seek rising zones of warm air called "thermals." The pilot then circles within the thermal and they are lifted up as if they were in an elevator. Strong thermals can easily lift a hang glider 3,000 feet (915m). The pilot can then seek out additional thermals for added lift, or fly around until they require a further thermal to once again get to higher altitude.

Improvements to the design of hang gliders stemming from the Rogallo Wing and other technological advances, have spawned a tremendous rise in the popularity of hang gliding. Basically, these improvements have created hang gliders that are easier to fly, more comfortable, and much harder to crash.

Before some of the modern teaching techniques were developed, students had to struggle through a trial and error learning process and were forced to attempt new maneuvers cold. Flying a hang glider requires familiarizing oneself with the feel of each maneuver, which can often prove to be a long, difficult, and sometimes painful process. It is

Launch is from a running start, generating the initial lift needed for flight.

this factor that used to discourage many from pursuing the sport.

Learning to hang glide has become far easier with the introduction of tandem training techniques. Tandem training allows a qualified instructor to fly with their trainee and demonstrate new maneuvers in real-time, allowing students to get the "feel" of a move without having to master it first. It is estimated that this technique can shorten the learning curve for hang gliders by as much as 30 per cent. One of the principal reasons for the shortened curve is that tandem instruction allows beginners to experience and get the feel of even the most intricate maneuvers without the need to master hang gliding first.

Once a beginner has learned to hang glide solo, they start out flying beginner "ships" that are much less streamlined than performance versions. These beginner models are far more forgiving, allowing for some pilot error while skills are developed. Once they've learned the nuances of hang gliding flight, they are no longer considered to be a "wuffo," which in hang gliding circles means a bad pilot or someone who knows nothing about the sport.

Hang gliders are deceptively strong. They are built of aircraft quality aluminum and stainless steel with a sail (the wing) generally made of dacron. The structure is held together by a series of wires that create an amazingly stable geometry. A typical hang glider is capable of handling a load of over one ton without breaking. Today's hang glider technology allows them to be outfitted with full instrumentation, radios, and even rocket deployed emergency parachutes.

For those readers who wish to try their hand at hang gliding, look to your local organizations who can provide you with training manuals, videos, and where to get proper instruction. I have always dreamt of hang gliding, and hope to soon get out and do it.

Tandem flight in the mountains.

Once airborne, the pilot looks to find 'thermals' - rising zones of warm air - on which to gain altitude.

Ski Jumping & Ski Flying

Pointing your skis downhill as fast as you can is something that millions of us do every year when taking in any one of several ski resorts or cross country touring centers around the globe. Each skier has sought out a bump or jump from time to time, and all can appreciate the rush that even a small launch into the air can provide. That thrill has driven skiers to seek jumps for as long as there have been skis.

The "V" style, currently the state-of-the-art of ski jumping.

IN THE SMALL TOWN of Telemark, Norway, Sondre Norheim revolutionized skiing when he developed the loose heel binding system for nordic (cross country) skiers in 1861. The "telemark" turn and style of nordic skiing was born from the techniques Sondre developed, and soon accomplished nordic skiers began building small jumps to test their skills.

The first nordic skiing and jumping contests are believed to have been held in 1892.

The first dedicated jumping hill was built in Oslo in that same year. That location is still host to the annual Holmenkollen Ski Festival.

As Norwegians began emigrating to other countries, most notably the U.S. and Canada, they brought their nordic skills with them, and nordic skiing and jumping competitions gained a new base of enthusiasts. In 1924, Ski Jumping was included in the first Winter Olympics. The "Nordic Combined" Olympic medals are awarded to athletes competing for best in the world honors for combined cross country racing and ski jumping ability to this day.

As ski jumping matured, many techniques were created in an effort to travel the

At take off point the hill is not flat, but sloped downwards at 11 degrees.

32

maximum distance possible. A scoring system for jumps was created that considered not only distance but also style for each jumper. Over time, jumping styles included "windmilling" their arms while in flight, stretching their arms forward until landing, leaning over their skis in a jack-knife position, and finally the modern "V" style. Each style was considered state of the art for its time.

As ski jumping styles changed, so did the skis themselves, gradually becoming longer and wider. Modern jumping skis average 8ft 2in–8ft 10in (2.50-2.65m) in length and are roughly twice the width of traditional nordic skis. As the skis got longer and wider, they added lift to the skier, thus making for longer and longer jumps.

Finding the lift

Olympic Ski Jumping hills have traditionally measured 90 and 120 meters (300 and 395 feet). The rating is based on the distance from the jump to the "K-Point" on the hill. The K-Point is the point at which the hill begins its transition to a flat surface. To illustrate this measurement, a 90-meter jump has a K-Point that is 90 meters from the jump, a 120-meter jump has a K-Point that is 120 meters... and so on. As ski jumping equipment enabled jumpers to clear the K-Point by greater and greater distances, a new K-Point was needed.

The new K-Point was established at 140 meters (460 feet), and the sport of ski jumping became the sport of ski flying. The basic techniques are the same for ski flying as ski jumping. Today, the most frequently used technique is the "V" style in which the skier points their skis so that the tails are nearly touching, and the tips are wide apart, creating a V shape. With the "V" style, skiers are able to use the additional lift the position offers, and fly a trajectory that keeps them only 10 feet (3m) above the slope below them, versus older techniques that could have the skier hovering 20 or more feet above the slope.

Flying the jump

To jump, the skier starts down the hill to the jump site from a seated position high above the take off point. Skiers crouch down to optimize their aerodynamic form and minimize wind resistance. In this position, they accelerate to speeds exceeding 60 mph (96kph) before reaching their take off point. At the take-off point, the skiers lunge

Such a spectacular view is the province of only the top class ski jumpers in the world.

The thrill of off-piste ski jumping has inspired the sports of Ski Jumping and Ski Flying.

forward toward the tips of their skis, adding the final lift-generating form, their body. The take off point is not flat, but sloped downward at 11 degrees.

On landing, the skier uses a traditional telemark-style position, with one foot in front of the other. In that position, the front foot is flat with the knee bent, and the back heel is slightly elevated with the knee low and bent. This is the correct landing position for both ski jumping and ski flying.

Each jump is scored based on the style of the jump from take-off to the landing, and the distance traveled relative to the K-Point. Style points are awarded by a panel of five judges. Each can award up to 20 points for style. The highest and lowest scores are discarded, and the sum of the remaining scores is the skier's style total. Therefore, the maximum style points available to a jumper is 60.

Distance points based on the K-Point are added or subtracted based on a predetermined scale and are given in meter and half-meter increments. Skiers reaching the K-Point are automatically awarded 60 points. Distances beyond or short of the K-Point add or subtract from the overall distance score. Distance points are added to style points, and a winner is chosen. The current distance world record is held by Norwegian Espen Bredsen, who flew 209 meters (686ft).

Galondee Jumping

One of the less structured extreme ski jumping styles is referred to as galondee. In galondee jumping, skiers jump for distance using traditional alpine skiing equipment. Alpine skis use a fixed heel and toe binding system with rigid boots. Alpine skiing is the style generally practiced at ski resorts using lift-served terrain.

Galondee jumps are not nearly as long distance as ski jumping or flying using nordic equipment, since the fixed heel limits the skier's ability to generate lift. While galondee jumping can be done on ski jumping hills, it is often done in natural settings using steep hills with bumps and drop offs that are available. Galondee jumping competitions do exist, however, the spirit of most events is less structured than galondee jumping's Olympic counterparts.

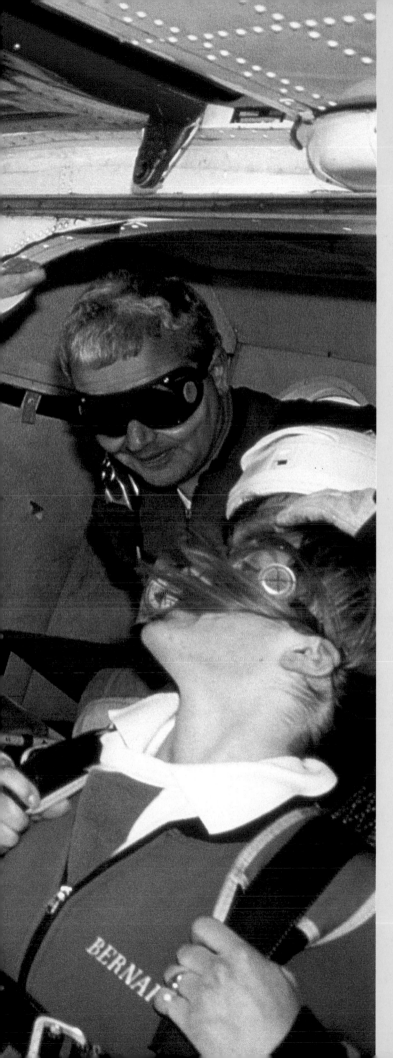

Sky Diving

Free-falling from an aircraft is one of the extreme sports that millions around the world take part in every year. The excitement of plummeting to earth with the time to think and enjoy the view is what attracts so many to jump from what most would consider a perfectly good airplane. Over the years, sky diving has evolved from what was once a necessary skill of self preservation to the source of inspiration for other sports like sky surfing and B.A.S.E. jumping.

Stacked canopy formation sky diving is a popular aspect of the sport today.

Having progressed through the learning stages (generally 15-plus jumps), new sky divers are ready to try more difficult maneuvers and tests of skill. With practice, they can soon participate in the sport of sky diving, including events like accuracy contests, formation free fall, canopy stacking, canopy relative work, freestyle, and perhaps even sky surfing and

OVER THE YEARS, the high standards developed for both jump schools and jumping operations have made sky diving a relatively safe sport. According to the United States Parachuting Association, during the last five years, only one jump in 80,000 has resulted in death, suggesting that sky diving may well be safer than driving a car in many places.

Traditionally, sky diving students have been taught by the "static line" method which automatically deploys the jumper's chute once clear of the aircraft. This method allows for no free fall time, so most schools are moving to the tandem and Accelerated Free Fall methods of instruction. In a tandem jump, the student can experience the thrill of free fall while safely connected to a certified instructor. The AFF method then allows the student to jump solo and free fall in the company of instructors, who free fall with the student until they successfully deploy their chute.

Another benefit of the evolution of sky diving is the development of the square "Ram Air"-style parachute which allows jumpers to steer their chutes and provides additional lift compared to the older round chutes. The additional lift makes for a softer landing, too.

B.A.S.E. jumping if they're so inclined.

Shortly before WWI, the idea of parachuting for sport was born when bi-plane tours became a popular attraction at fairs. In 1930, the first known parachuting contest was held in Russia. Contestants were scored on their ability to hit a ground target. Target accuracy is an aspect of parachuting competition that is still practiced today. Present day targets are merely 20 inches (0.5m) in diameter. The current record for accuracy is held by Russian sky diver Linger Abdurakhmanov, who landed on the target disk an incredible 50 consecutive times.

Formation free fall events take place when several sky divers free fall together, then move into positions enabling them to hold on to one and other in formation. The danger of formation free fall stems from the possibility of a high-speed collision mid-air, causing one or more jumpers to lose consciousness. The use of an Automatic Deployment Device (ADD) is one way to ensure that unconsciousness does not lead to a non-deployment. The current World Record for Free

Canopy Relative Work events consist of 2 or more people making geometric shapes in their jumps, here 80 women try for the world record in France, 1990.

AFF jumping allows students and instructors to dive together.

"Ram-Air" parachutes allow sky divers more lift and flexibility in their descent.

Fall Formation is held by 200 sky divers who managed to link up over Myrtle Beach, South Carolina in 1992.

Another style of formation jumping occurs after deployment. In stacked canopy formation sky diving, the jumpers deploy their chutes and then physically hook their legs into the lines of the open canopy of a jumper below. Another series of jumpers then stack themselves on the canopies of the linked jumpers, until the final formation is completed.

The biggest risk in this form of formation sky diving is that the jumpers can get entangled in the canopies of other jumpers with deadly results. Jumpers all carry secondary canopies in case they must cut themselves free of entanglement. The current World Record was set in 1994 when 46

jumpers fell into a stacked canopy formation over Davis, California. The canopy relative work (CPW) event consists of two or more sky divers working together to form geometric formations. Geometric forms are created through aerial maneuvers that are judged.

Dancing in the sky

Freestyle sky diving is an aerial ballet that is captured on camera for judging. The freestyle sky diver performs an assortment of airborne gymnastic maneuvers prior to deploying their chute, and is judged on the style and artistic elements of the jump.

The sport of sky diving has an interesting history. There are reports of parachute-like devices being used in 12th century China as well as 16th century

Venice. The first documented use of a parachute was in 1783, the same year balloons were first being experimented with. A large audience in Paris watched as stunt performer Andre Germain jumped with a parachute in 1797. In 1808, Jodaki Kuparento bailed out of a burning balloon several thousand feet above Warsaw in the first documented emergency use of a parachute. He survived.

Of course, most of the styles of sky diving would not be possible had Frenchman Leo Valentin not developed a technique for

stabilized free fall in 1948. The fact that sky divers could free fall for prolonged periods under control is what led to the establishment of much of the modern sky diving elements. The first Parachuting World Championships were held shortly thereafter in 1951 in the former Yugoslavia.

The sport of sky diving is one of the easiest of the extreme sports to learn, and dive centers are located in every major region of the world. Anyone considering learning should seek out a center with new equipment and a history of quality instruction.

Sky surfer and camera-flyer - travelling at speeds of up to 120 mph (197kph) - are involved in a high-speed synchronized free fall ballet.

Sky Surfing

Parachutists have long experimented with different ways of using their bodies to steer them through the air during free fall. By stretching out in a horizontal fashion, sky divers found they could zoom about in different directions at remarkable speeds with quite a bit of directional control. It was, of course, simply a matter of time until someone tried free falling using a flat surface that could add to their speed, control, and push the limits of what had been done.

FIRST, AS EARLY AS 1980, a few skydivers in California started testing free fall while lying on top of boogie boards. These pioneers found that the boards added some speed and directional control but, most importantly, proved that jumping with boards could be done.

Next, Frenchman Joel Cruciani jumped while standing on a small surfboard which had been modified by mounting snowboard bindings to it. Joel strapped in and became the first skysurfer, a stunt that was featured in the film *Hibernator*. This board was reportedly unstable and difficult to surf on due to the size of the surface he needed to control in flight.

In 1988, another French sky diver, by the name of Laurent Bouquet, began experimenting with boards for free fall. His design used a skateboard-sized board that strapped to his feet. It was obviously much smaller than Cruciani's, and very easily controlled.

In 1989, yet another Frenchman, expert B.A.S.E. jumper and extreme parachutist the late Patrick de Gayardon, designed and perfected a binding cut-away system that allowed a sky surfer to release the board should he lose control in free fall. The addition of this binding system provided the opportunity for sky surfers to experiment with a number of shapes and sizes, evolving to the snowboard shape that is the favorite of most sky surfers. Later that year, de Gayardon portrayed the "Silver Surfer" for film-maker Thierry Donard's *Pushing the Limits 2*.

By 1990, the Silver Surfer inspired other European jumpers to try sky surfing. Soon news spread throughout the sky diving world of this new and exciting sport, and the stage was set for its exponential growth over the next six years. Many new tricks evolved as the sky surfers pushed the limits of their sport.

The flying eye

In the fall of 1990. the World Freestyle Federation (WFF) staged the first World Freestyle Championships in Texas, and introduced sky surfing as a featured demonstration. The 1990 World Freestyle Championships marked the first time that the "team video concept" was used. WFF founder Pete Mckeeman was the first to envision using a "camera-flyer" to capture a sky surfer's performance for judging purposes. Sky surfing instantly became a made-for-TV sport, accelerating the already rapid growth.

The introduction of a free-falling, cameraman partner into sky surfing created an entirely new series of complications. The highly maneuverable sky surfer is capable of traveling at speeds that can exceed 120 mph (193kph) in many directions during free fall. The cameraman also travels downward at similar speeds. Should the two collide the result can be unconsciousness or worse. Therefore, sky surfers and their cameraman partners use an AAD, or Auto Activation Device. The auto-deployment takes place at a predetermined altitude or time to prevent non-deployment in the case of injury or loss of consciousness. Sky surfers also run the risk of spinning out of control, in which case the AAD also proves invaluable.

In competition, a sky surfer and cameramen are scored as a team. With team video scoring it is the overall presentation that is judged. How the camera-flyer positions himself during free fall, how he frames his shots, and how in-synch he can stay with the sky surfer all factor into the score.

The resulting footage and the sport itself have evolved into a highly synchronized free fall ballet—with the sky surfer and camera-flyer executing simultaneous rolls, flips, and spins while hurtling toward the ground at around 120 mph. Winning teams display a coherence and consistency of movement between the sky surfer and the cameraman that is uncanny. At larger competitions, a direct feed from the camera-flyer's camera to a "jumbotron" monitor on the ground allows spectators to see the performance in real-time.

Sky surfing is very exciting to watch. For those wishing to try their hand at it, this is a sport to be left to only the very best and most experienced sky divers. For example, two time Sky Surfing World Champion Joe Jennings was killed in 1996 while sky surfing for a commercial in California, reportedly victim to a partial deployment.

Soaring

Soaring is a rush that can be realized by just about anyone. If the thought of quietly flying through the clouds with the agility of a bird is appealing, it can be done easily and inexpensively. There is no need to bruise yourself learning, for it's as easy as finding a soaring center where you can rent a ride.

BY DEFINITION, soaring and gliding are different, although they are commonly used terms to describe the sport of soaring. Soaring is defined as flying without engine power and without loss of altitude. Gliding on the other hand, is defined as flying without engine power, and a glider is a aircraft without a power source.

Gliders are towed from airfields by towplanes using tow ropes of between 150–200 feet (45–60m) in length. The tow ropes are light, stretchy, abrasion-resistant lines with high strength-to-weight ratios. Tow ropes are designed to be dropped by the glider once the desired altitude has been achieved. The glider is then left to the task of finding ways in which to increase its altitude without assistance.

Gliders all have a "Glide Ratio" which refers to how many feet the craft can glide compared to the altitude that it loses in flight. So, a glide ratio of 22:1 would signify that the glider is capable of traveling 22 feet for every 1 foot it loses in altitude.

A glide ratio of 22:1 is normal for many of today's gliders, such as the Schweizer 2-33, one

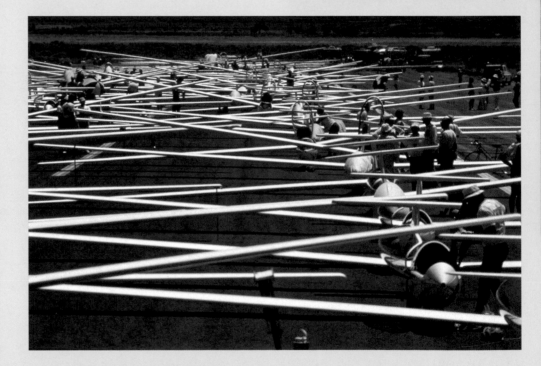

of the most popular training gliders in the world. Gliders like the Schweizer have maximum speeds of around 100mph (160kph). There are many high performance gliders with ratios in excess of 50:1 that are capable of speeds exceeding 110 mph (176kph).

Of course once you have defined the glide ratio, you know how far your glider can fly before it reaches the ground. The object of soaring is to use rising warm air currents, or

"thermals", to lift the glider at rates equal to or in excess of their glide ratio. Each time the pilot catches a thermal and rides it upward, they extend both the distance they can travel and the duration of their flight.

Understanding and being able to read the air currents in a search for thermals is where the art of soaring begins. It is also where the sport of soaring is derived. Much of soaring hinges on the pilot's ability to travel specific

distances, reach predetermined locations, or pass through specific zones, maximize or minimize total time spent aloft, and a mixture of these tasks. The trick to winning is utilizing the thermals to reach your performance goals.

Reading thermals is no easy task. They are invisible, yet they can be found by reading the horizon and cloud patterns for clues to their existence. Top pilots are also sound meteorologists, who understand the meaning of cloud formations and the effects of solar radiant heating as the day progresses.

In 1964, Al Parker became the first glider pilot to fly 1,000 kilometers (621 miles) non-stop. In 1977, Karl Striedieck completed the first 1,000-mile (1,600-kilometer) non-

stop glider flight. Today, pilots continue to push the performance envelopes of their gliders. What seems to be the only barrier to the next record is technological advances in materials that can make the gliders lighter and faster with increased glide ratios.

Reaching for the sky

If you're wondering who started it all, you can thank Sir George Cayley, who flew the first manned glider in 1853. Since that day, soaring and glider technology have come a long way. Eventually the gliders were modified to be airplanes, which were modified to be towplanes, which gliders still use today to take off and gain their initial altitude.

After WWI, the first modern soaring competition was held in Wasserkuppe, Germany in 1920. In 1921, the first soaring flight using thermals to ascend was made by Wolfgang Klemperer. The Germans went on to perfect virtually all of the important soaring equipment and techniques used today.

Soaring is certainly an exciting and challenging sport that can be enjoyed by virtually anyone seeking the thrill of powerless flight and the challenge of staying aloft using the natural forces of the wind and sun.

Land
Sports

There are many natural elements we refer to as land that can be extreme and particularly challenging for survival, nevermind the pursuit of sport.

FURTHER INFORMATION

BIBLIOGRAPHY

- *Land Sailing*, Scott Robert Hays, Capstone Press, Mankato, Minnesota, 1992
- *Olympic Nordic Skiing*, By the Staff of the Ice Skating Institute of America in cooperation with the U.S. Olympic Committee, Children's Press, Chicago, Illinois, 1979
- *The Triathlon Training and Racing Book*, Sally Edwards, Contemporary Books, Inc., Chicago, Illinois, 1985
- *Rock & Mountain Climbing*, Ruth and John Mendenhall, Stackpole Books, Harrisburg, PA, 1983
- *Mock Rock The Guide To Indoor Climbing*, Sharon Colette Urquhart, Paper Chase Press, New Orleans, Louisiana, 1995
- *The Handbook of Motocross*, Jerry Murray, G. P. Putnam's Sons, New York, 1978

ASSOCIATIONS & CLUBS

AGGRESSIVE INLINE SKATING
- Aggressive Skaters Association
  13468 Beach Avenue
  Marina del Ray
  CA 90292
  Tel: (001) 310-823-1865
  Fax: (001) 310-823-4146
- International Inline Skating Association
  105 South 7th Street
  Wilmington
  NC 28401
  Tel: (001) 910-762-7004
  Fax: (001) 910-762-9477
- US Amateur Confederation of
  Roller Skates (inline)
  4730 South St.
  PO Box 6579 Lincoln, NE 68506
  Tel: (001) 402-483-7551

BMX
- American Bicycle Association
  9831 S. 51st St., Suite D135
  Phoenix, AZ 85044, also
  PO Box 718
  Chandler, AZ 85244
  Tel: (001) 602-961-1903
  Fax: (001) 602-961-1842
- International Amateur Cycling Federation
  Via Cassia 490I-00189, Rome, Italy
  Tel: (0039) 6-331-2419
  Fax: (0039) 6-331-0079

CAVING
- International Subterranean
  secretariat de j'AIPS, 94 Rue de la Culée
  B-6927 Resteigne, Belgium
  Tel: (0032) 84 38 82 26
  Fax: (0032) 84 38 82 32
- National Caving Association (UK)
  Monomark House, 27 Old Gloucester St.,
  London WC1N 3XX,
- National Speleological Society (U.S.)
  2813 Cave Ave
  Huntsville, Alabama 35810-4413

CLIMBING (INDOOR)
- Australian Indoor Climbing Index
  www.arapiles.com/cgi-
  bin/links.cgi?category=gyms
- Dutch Climbing Home Page
  www.climbing.nl
- U.S. Climbing Gym List
  www.dtek.chalmer.se/Climbing/
  Commercial/gymsUS.html

CLIMBING (OUTDOOR)
- American Alpine Club
  929 Pearl Street
  Suite 300
  Boulder, CO 80302
  Tel: (001) 303-443-6800
  Fax: (001)303-443-6864
- American Sport Climbers Federation
  125 W. 96th St., #1D
  New York, New York 10025
  Tel: (001) 212-865-4383
  Fax: (001) 212-865-4383
- *Climbing* (magazine)
  1101 Village Rd, Suite LL-1-B
  Carbondak, CO 81623
  Tel: (001) 970-963-9449
- *Rock and Ice* (magazine)
  www.rockandice.com

CONSIDER THE DESERTS, mountains, and glaciers that cover much of our planet. These landscapes have secured borders and civilizations over the centuries. A would-be conqueror whose forces lacked desert survival or mountaineering skills would be ill advised to try to beat the elements and his enemy at the same time. Recent history in Afghanistan shows that an understanding of survival skills and terrain can resist even a high-tech invader.

We are fortunate that extreme sports are not about conquering others, only the limitations of the athlete's mind, body, and equipment. Most land-based extreme sports take place in areas that would have hardly been considered hospitable a century ago. Thanks to technology, we can now travel to, and play in, these places in relative comfort. However, technology has not changed the landscape of the harshest elements, or the skill sets necessary to survive in them.

Technology and change have created some new landscapes. The urban elements are the endless miles of pavement, the stairs made from cement and stone and the railings affixed to them. As with the natural elements, the urban elements bring with them a new set of challenges and opportunities for sport. The urbanscape is also more accessible than natural elements. As a result, urban extreme sports are the ones most likely to satisfy athletes who can't play in the natural elements due to either time or money.

PUSHING THE LIMITS

It was the existence of each of these elements that spawned each extreme sport, not the harshness of the landscapes or the number of

man-made obstacles that have been created. It was, to paraphrase legendary explorer and mountaineer Sir Edmund Hillary, "because they were there." This was more than just a witty statement. In this phrase is the soul and the spirit of extreme pursuit. Hillary did not ascend Mount Everest because he needed to for survival. He did so to push his limits physically and mentally.

Extreme athletes look at the landscape differently than "normal" people. Climbers traveling through mountainous regions look at the series of potential routes on each face as they pass by. "Normal" folk simply see nice mountains. Skateboarders and inline skaters walk through a city park and see the flora and fauna, but tend to focus on the curbs, stairs, and railings as personal challenges to their technical abilities. "Normal" folks walk through parks and see only the birds and squirrels.

Land-based extreme sports have the greatest diversity of terrain. Each sport requires the athlete be able to ascend, descend, jump, and coast through any number of circumstances and unexpected obstacles. Quick reflexes and absolute focus quickly separate the best from the simply good.

TESTING OURSELVES

It is difficult to envision what the next extreme sport to be born will be as we redraw our urban landscapes and develop new materials that will allow us to redefine performance and perhaps better survive the harsher elements. As man and technology change and improve, our ability to test ourselves within our natural and urban environments will change. Extreme athletes seeking to push their limits will adapt new technology and thinking, creating new opportunities for future extreme athletes to redefine how to have fun on the planet.

ACW Climbing

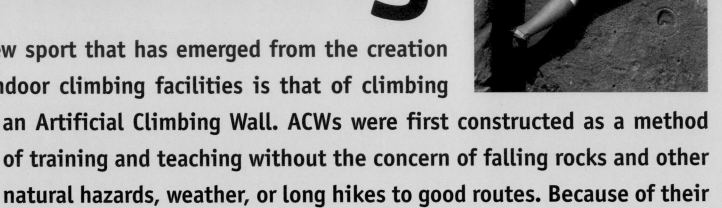

A new sport that has emerged from the creation of indoor climbing facilities is that of climbing an Artificial Climbing Wall. ACWs were first constructed as a method of training and teaching without the concern of falling rocks and other natural hazards, weather, or long hikes to good routes. Because of their easy access in urban areas, ACWs have become a major draw at gyms.

ACWS HAVE ENABLED an entire group of athletes, who may not have ever been exposed to climbing, to get a taste and, if hooked, to learn substantial skill sets before ever venturing out to a real rock face. The same skills of balance, stance, and movement needed on rock and ice (crampon and ice axe use excluded) are required to climb walls, and with the many new materials and modular construction techniques, ACWs can recreate any level of climb desired, except for constraints on the height of the climb that natural settings don't have. ACWs aid both experienced climbers and those new to the sport to achieve the flexibility, finesse, and strength required as well as allowing them to maintain the commitment to the sport that top climbers must have to be successful.

Climbing competitions are judged on the basis of a climber's ability to get through difficult routes without falling, and the speed at which the climber is able to ascend the wall. There are categories for both speed and difficulty in most competitions. International climbing competitions on ACWs have been organized since 1987 when the former Soviet Union began holding speed climbing events. The first World Championships were held in 1991 in Frankfurt, Germany, allowing the International Olympic Committee to offer the sport Olympic status that same year.

The difficulty of competitions is judged by determining the highest point on the route each competitor reaches within a set period of time. Each climber must climb the route "on-sight," without seeing the route before their climb, and without witnessing others attempting it.

Speed events are held on easier routes and are normally held in a double-elimination-style format, with two climbers racing simultaneously. The first to complete the route wins that heat. Losing two heats eliminates a climber from the event.

The wall at the World Speed Climbing Championships in Birmingham, England.

Substantial climbing skills can be learned on ACWs - balance, stance and movement on both rock and ice - the same skills required in the real world outside.

Karen Smyers of the U.S.A. in winning action in the Ironman, Kona, Hawaii, 1995.

Adventure Racing

Mark Allen, looks cool during the Ironman marathon, 1995.

Teamwork is essential for success in the Raid Gauloises, Argentina 1995.

I doubt many people would argue that triathlons are not grueling tests of an athlete's physical conditioning and mental toughness. For the unfamiliar, triathlons are events where competitors face off in a combination of swimming, biking, and a running race. Triathlons vary considerably from venue to venue. The original triathlon and the triathlon most deserving of the word extreme is the Ironman, an event that draws the world's top triathletes from 75 countries to Hawaii each year in October.

Whitewater action, Raid Gauloises, Borneo, 1994

WHAT MAKES THE IRONMAN the most extreme triathlon is not its distance—many world class triathlons have similar distances—it is the weather. Temperatures, with highs averaging 88°F (31°C) and humidity levels between 40–85 per cent, are sometimes accompanied by 60 mph (97 kph) winds. Athletes can expect to endure conditions that make this one event more torturous than most.

The Ironman got its start in 1978, when Navy Commander John Collins created a race based on three existing races: The Waikiki Rough Water Swim of 2.4 miles (3.9km), the Around Oahu Bike Race of 112 miles (180 km), and the Honolulu Marathon of 26.2 miles (42.2km). The first Ironman took place on Kialua, but was moved after three years to Kona to avoid the traffic around Honolulu.

At the back of beyond

Another race that can hardly be deemed anything less than extreme is the Raid Gauloises, an event that got its start as a ten-day, 400-mile (644 km) stage race conceived

The unexpected is always expected in the Raid, Borneo 1994.

by French journalist Gérard Fusil. The race takes place in a different area of extreme outback each year, such as Madagascar, Borneo, and Patagonia.

The Raid Gauloises participants are five-person teams from various countries sponsored by a variety of corporations. The teams race up and down 14,000-foot (4,267m) mountains, through swamps and down rivers, taking a massive toll on the team members, both physically and mentally. Each team member must complete the race for their team to be scored as finished. The Raid is a survivalist's dream race, arguably calling on more mental toughness than any other race in the world. This is clearly not a weekend warriors endeavor.

To find a new threat

The Raid Gauloises has given birth to a new adventure racing trend, with several aspiring adventure races establishing themselves, including the Eco-Challenge Series promoted by *Survivor* producer Englishman Mark Burnett, a former Raid participant. The Eco-Challenge has established itself as the foremost adventure race in the world, attracting a wide range of participants as well as global television coverage.

Adventure racing in many ways appears to be a response to life in a world largely protected from threats to survival and the necessity of pioneering new frontiers.

It is easy to draw parallels between what these teams are doing for sport and what mankind has done for centuries to redefine our borders. The major difference today is that should we run into a life-threatening problem during one of these events, a heli-lift to safety is not far off.

Best all-arounder

In fact, most adventure races now employ the use of hand-held GPS (Global Positioning Satellite) systems that not only enable the competitors to establish where they are within a few meters, but also enable rescuers to find them quickly if need be. There are devices called sextants, once used to navigate the seas and land by reading the stars, but they can be rendered useless by clouds, and can only be read by those holding them, and not those seeking to offer rescue.

Adventure racing draws from many different extreme sports: climbing, whitewater, and mountain biking for example.

Surely event organizers and creators will find ways of including more and more extreme sports in their events until a decathlon style event is created which will act to find the best all-around extreme sports athlete in the world.

53

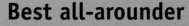
A spectacular start of the swimming race at the Gatorade Ironman in Kona, Hawaii.

The physical and mental toll on team members in the Raid separates the winners from the losers, Borneo 1994.

Aggressive Inline Skating

The ground broken by skateboarders over the past three decades has been invaded by a new group of urban athletes. Aggressive inline skaters have co-opted much of the style and culture of skateboarding into their sport. Aggressive skaters have taken what were initially just fitness and training devices and transformed them into urban assault vehicles that have been embraced by pop culture.

INLINE SKATES CAN TRACE their roots back to the Chicago Skate Company, and perhaps further, as evidence of wheeled boots dates back to the early days of bicycling. But it wasn't until brothers Scott and Brennan Olsen created the first Rollerblades in their Minneapolis basement in 1979, that the sport took off. The brothers stumbled on a pair of Chicago Skate Company's inline skates in the bargain bin of a used equipment store while looking for a way to train for hockey in the off season. The skates offered minimal support and awful wheels. The Olsens added greater support and urethane wheels, and the rest is history.

Scott Olsen bought the patent for inline skates from the Chicago Skate Company and began the Rollerblade Company. The first Rollerblades were nothing more than hockey boots with an inline chassis. By 1983, Scott Olsen sold Rollerblade to Robert Nagle, Jr. With new capital resources, new and improved Rollerblades were developed, and the beginning of a growth curve unparalleled in the sporting goods industry had begun.

At first, the Rollerblade inline skates were designed to provide cross-training for hockey skaters. Then skiers discovered that Rollerblades offered the ability to get a carved-turn sensation on pavement, and

This competitor at the 1997 Headworx Championships has no time to admire the scenery.

became the second major group to used inline skates for cross-training. Inline skates soon became a heavily promoted and endorsed method for training in the off season within the ski industry.

The third and largest group to embrace the Rollerblade phenomenon was the Eighties' aerobic and fitness crowd. Fitness fanatics quickly recognized that skating was a great way to tone the legs and buttocks while increasing aerobic capacity with far lower impact than running. By 1989, over three million inline skates were being sold each year. By 1994, the U.S. National Sporting Goods Association estimated there were over twelve million inline skaters in the U.S. alone.

Prepared for anything

Soon the boom in inline skating reciprocated in reported injuries from falls. Most common were broken wrists, arms, and head injuries. This prompted an aggressive effort to teach skaters to protect themselves properly by wearing wrist, elbow, knee, and head protection when skating. Use of these items has greatly reduced the risks of injury in a fall. Smart skaters, whether skating for fitness or trick skating, have all found these items work well when needed.

Naturally, it was only a matter of time before the top inline skaters would seek to redefine their sport. No longer content to skate about town in a "civilized" manner, top skaters began to search for a new, less aerobic and fitness oriented identity. The new breed of aggressive skaters turned to the skateboard world for guidance, not only for cultural grounding but for a direction to push their sport forward. In turn, this gave way to "street style" and "vert" inline skating.

Street skating

Like skateboarding, "street" inline skaters seek to jump over and grind across just about any obstacle imaginable. To do so requires special grind plates attached to the chassis of the skates, so that the wheels don't grab at inappropriate times, and the skate's chassis aren't destroyed by the moves. These needs wound up giving birth to an entire sub-industry created to serve the needs of aggressive skaters that the corporate manufactures are only now recognizing represent the future of inline skating. Open an aggressive inline magazine like *Box* or *Daily Bread* and you'll find everything from over-sized pads to T-shirts to Titanium skate chassis. Grind plates, custom chassis, and specialized wheels and many of the items that aggressive skaters used to fashion for themselves are now available via mail order.

Vert skating began when inliners first invaded the sacred territory of skate-boarders, the half-pipe. At first, this invasion created tension at the skate parks, which in most places has died down as inliners have gotten better and now demand some respect for their abilities. Inline vert skating does differ in some ways from skateboarding vert, since the skater's feet are free to move independently. The skater who has had the most impact on technical independent foot moves presently is Australia's Matt Salerno. His abilities are redefining vert skating, creating maneuvers that are truly the property of the aggressive inline movement.

Special terms

Aggressive inline skaters have created a number of terms to define the moves they make, both on the street and when skating vert. ABEC is an acronym for Annular Bearing Engineering Council. ABEC ratings correspond to the speed and efficiency of the bearing sets which can be replaced, removed, cleaned, and reinserted into the wheel sets. The higher the rating (between 1–5) the faster the bearing will roll.

The durometer figure is how wheels are gauged for hardness. The higher the durometer number, the harder the wheel.

Rockering is the process of lowering or raising the middle two wheels or outside two wheels to create either a flat or curved skate contact with the surface being ridden. A curved rocker allows for quicker turning while a flatter rocker allows for greater stability, especially at speed.

Spacers are small round tubes that are used to separate the bearings in each wheel and create a protective barrier between the bearing and the axle. Chassis refers to the plastic, metal, or composite frame that is secured to the bottom of each boot and which holds the wheel sets. Designs can vary greatly. If you wear the best gear to look the part but can't skate to save your life, you'll be referred to as a "poser."

Cheese Grater Asphalt is poor or rough road conditions or surfaces. Bail-To Fall is an intentional fall to avoid a nastier wipe out, and Slam Tan refers to tan lines caused by wearing the protective elbow, wrist, and knee protection.

However, there will always be those who don't want to be organized, and just want to hang out and do stuff.

56

Like skateboarding, street inline skaters seek to jump and grind over anything they can find, however inappropriate it may look to other people.

BMX

Just about every kid has attempted to jump their bike off something when they were growing up. Those that didn't certainly never became extreme sport athletes. The small and cruiser-style bikes of the Sixties and Seventies began a shift in how people viewed bicycle riding. Kids found that they were quite maneuverable, and the smaller wheels and fatter rubber tires made them more capable of enduring the thrashing a hard-riding kid could deliver. These new bikes redefined what could be done, and soon kids jumping things found they could jump bigger things, and could ride on softer surfaces, and the idea of dirt racing and jumping just kind of evolved naturally.

BICYCLE MOTOCROSS was born in Southern California in the Seventies, when organizers first began setting up weekend races on special dirt tracks resembling miniature motocross circuits. BMX dirt racing quickly grew into a national, and then international phenomenon. BMX racing went through a period when it was overlooked as the mountain bike craze hit, but it is now resurging, and many of today's mountain biking and motoX stars are former and current BMX racers.

BMX racing is organized to create ways for kids to compete safely and consistently. BMX now has local racing organizations in virtually every corner of the civilized world, and the impact on kids seeking a constructive outlet for their energy has been tremendous. Kids as young as five years old

In the Eighties vert riding in a half-pipe became the cutting edge of BMX. Today's top riders, like Matt Hoffman, have taken their tricks to new heights since then.

are encouraged to compete, and age categories ensure that kids compete against others of similar physical and skill levels. Pro BMX racing is not a kids' sport, however. The top pros are in their early- to late-twenties, paid well, and the business of BMX is to win.

Big and dirty air

By the Eighties, BMX had progressed beyond the limitations of the track. Riders seeking to push their limits and redefine what could be done on a 20-inch (51cm) bike pioneered trick riding, which included rolling tricks on a flat surface, called "flat land," and gravity-driven tricks in a half-pipe, called "vert" riding. Another outgrowth of BMX racing is the

With BMX now more popular than ever, BMX racing tracks are in short supply and a great addition to any community.

"big air dirt" jumping, where riders go fast and high while pulling off mid-air stunts for style with friends, or points in competition.

Flatland riding resembles a kind of pavement ballet, where riders stand and step over and around their bike frames while the bike is moving. Foot pegs are added to the front and rear axles of the bikes to give riders additional places for their feet while doing moves. The addition of foot pegs allows riders to spin their bikes around beneath them and perform other balance tricks they could not do otherwise.

America's Jamie Bestwick demonstrates incredible balance and control in his vert riding maneuvers.

Here are some vert riding maneuvers:

- **540** – spinning 540 degrees while above the coping.
- **900** – spinning 900 degrees while above the coping — very few pros can do it.
- **TAIL WHIP** – holding the handlebars and spinning the bike 360 degrees beneath you while above the coping.
- **PEG GRIND** – sliding the bike on both grind pegs on the coping.
- **FEEBLE PEG GRIND** – sliding one peg while rolling the other wheel on the coping.
- **FAKIE GRIND** – peg grind on coping moving backward.
- **BACK FLIP** – doing a back flip above the coping and landing.
- **FAKIE BAR SPIN** – spinning the handlebars while above the coping.

- **NAC NAC** – kicking one leg over and across the top tube while above the coping.
- **SUPERMAN AIR** – letting both feet fly away with the body outstretched above the coping.
- **LEAN AIR** – getting the rider's bike and body horizontal above the coping.

Dirt jumping can be performed just about anywhere you can find dirt—and where you can't, look for other stuff to jump. Many riders look to vacant lots to build jumps, while others build "box" jumps and other ramps to get air. The object is to go big and do a stylish trick in the process. Many of the tricks, with the exception of coping moves, come straight out of vert riding (or is it the other way around?). Jumping stuff is one part of BMX that's been around as long as there have been bikes.

Vert riding also uses foot pegs, but here they are referred to as "grind" pegs, since they are used to do tricks on the half-pipe's coping, a 2.5-inch (63.5mm) diameter metal tube that sits on the top edge of every half-pipe. Vert riders perform most of their maneuvers well above the coping. Top pros are capable of launching their bikes upward of 10 feet (3m) above the coping, where they adjust the attitude of their bikes and reenter the half-pipe in the same way that a skateboarder or inline skater would.

All the moves

Vert riding has been impacted the most by Matt Hoffman, who at age 15 redefined what could be done in a half-pipe. Since then, "The Condor" has gone on to win the World Championships eight consecutive times. In addition to his wins, he also owns the World Record for a vertical jump, which he set by being towed behind a motorcycle into a 20-foot (6.09m) quarter-pipe (half of a half-pipe). He jumped an amazing 50 feet (15.24m) above the ground, and landed it. Matt burst his spleen from the g-forces at the bottom of the landing, and nearly died from massive blood loss, having not realized he'd injured himself until it was almost too late!

Flatland riding (top left) resembles a kind of pavement ballet and uses foot pegs added to the bike's axles. Dirt jumping (right), however, requires nothing more than some dirt, a bike, and if possible, an audience.

The top riders are highly-paid pros, usually in their early to late-twenties. The sport is most popular in the U.S. where it continues to expand its appeal.

Caving

Walking, scrambling on all fours, and crawling on your belly into the moist darkness of a cave is not everyone's idea of a good time, but it is certainly extreme. The labyrinth-like tunnels that can lead to huge sheer drop offs or expansive chasms are not for the faint of heart. Those prone to nightmares from watching too many reruns of Dracula also may not appreciate the propensity of caves to attract legions of bats.

APPROPRIATELY, those who do cave (serious cavers do not refer to their sport as spelunking or potholing) always travel to the inner depths of the earth in groups of two or more. Not surprisingly, cavers are subject to many dangers that one would expect could occur in a cave, such as death by starvation, falling, asphyxiation, drowning, and hypothermia from exposure.

Cavers navigate the subterranean routes with the use of lamps on their helmets. The lamps are either carbide-style, fueled by a jet of acetylene gas like in the old days of coal mining, or newer electric lighting systems using bulbs, batteries, and intermittent-pulsing lamp technologies. Having lights is so critical to a caver's survival that, as a rule, each caver should carry at least three independent sources of light with them

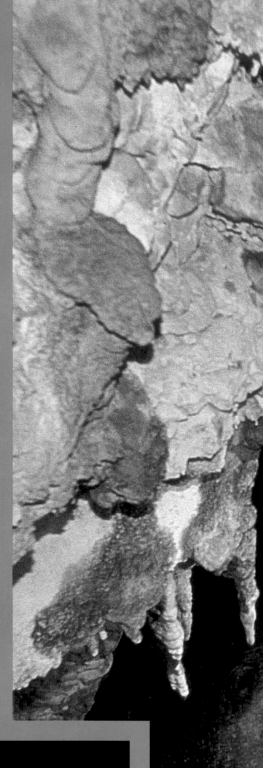

Cavers always travel to the inner depths of the earth in groups of two or more.

before entering any cave. Other equipment required for caving expeditions includes a helmet, kneepads, a small pack, good boots, gloves, and mental clarity, for a lack mental toughness can be as much to blame for caving accidents as fate.

Expert cavers can explore regions that require additional equipment such as wetsuits, rope, climbing gear for technical sections—such as chocks and harnesses for ascending and rapelling—cable ladders, and even scuba equipment.

Geological thrills

All cavers and aspiring cavers can reach the point at which they can explore truly extreme terrain, however, in order to get to that point, it is recommended that you join a grotto, which is a regional organization made up of cavers. Grottos are generally very helpful, and welcome new members and beginners as a way to grow their sport. Cavers are generally as interested in the historical and geological make up of the caves they trek as they are the thrill of traveling down into the damp darkness of the earth.

Once inside, caving requires most of the same technical skill that outdoor climbers use in the daylight. Some subterranean caverns are so extensive that they dwarf many frequently climbed outdoor climbing sites.

Caving is practiced globally, especially in regions that were once under water and so have the remains of aquatic creatures embedded in the earth which over geological time have turned to limestone. Most limestone is between 300 and 500 million years of age. In China, there are areas of limestone that can reach 2,000 feet (600m) in depth.

Caves offer tremendous historical evidence in some regions of the world. In France, for example, the famous Lascaux Caves have preserved drawings of prehistoric life, which now offer further insights into the origins of the human species. Similar evidence of man's history has been discovered in caves throughout the world.

Caving requires much of the same equipment needed for mountain climbing.

One of the main reasons caves offer so much evidence of history is that they provided shelter from enemies and storage for food and property that surface structures could not. Over the centuries, caves have also been useful places to stash loot and modern treasure hunters are still hard at work seeking to find the plunder.

Put it in, take it out

Caves, like the rest of the earth's treasures, are a limited and valuable resource, and a unique aspect of the global environment. There is a moral responsibility that all cavers

protect the caves they explore, minimizing the gradual deterioration that occurs once a cave is discovered.

One of caving's golden rules is that cavers take out of the cave everything that they bring in, since litter and pollution have already destroyed scientifically important caves across the globe. Even accidental damage can occur that prevents cave scientists from reconstructing evidence to get a better read on our history. As a result enthusiasts are now prohibited in many places from enjoying the natural beauty of the underground world.

It is essential that cavers take out everything they bring into the cave—this avoids destroying a unique and irreplaceable environment.

Top Freestyle Motocross rider Tommy Clowers looks as if he is getting an aerial tow from his bike at the X Games in San Francisco, California, but he has full control of his machine.

Freestyle Motocross

Today's best motocross machines, ranging from 125 and 250 two stroke models to new 400 plus four stroke designs, have pushed performances to their highest levels ever. Supercross tracks, with ultra steep takeoffs leading into double and triple jumps during competition, have placed a premium on aerial ability. Top Supercross riders, following the lead from eight-time champion Jeremy McGrath, began wowing crowds with a variety of stunts while launching distances exceeding 70 feet. Winning while performing big tricks became the mark of the best riders.

69

FREESTYLE TRICKS made their way into racing because top riders simply liked to push themselves on and off track while practising or simply riding for fun. And freestyle motocross looks like fun, especially if you can pull it off. Top riders began showcasing their antics in cult video productions like *Crusty Demons of Dirt*. These films spawned a cottage industry which appeals to a large, and growing, audience. The type of "reckless" behavior exhibited in these videos wasn't really new, the best riders have been pushing the limits of performance for as long as motocross has been around, they just didn't have the right equipment. The plots are simple, top caliber riders attempting phenomenal stunts.

Freestyle motocross is now considered a competition, with promoters successfully filling stadiums to witness the best challenge each other on a course built specifically for freestyle competition. Jumps spanning as far as 100 feet are constructed to allow the riders to get huge air and equally large hang time. While up there, competitors use the time to showcase their best tricks. As you might imagine, these attempts can lead to failure, and the resulting crashes can be spectacular if a bit painful for the rider.

Riders modify their bikes with handholds on the side and rear, allowing competitors to let go of their handlebars while still maintaining a grip on their ride. New stunts, previously impossible are now done regularly,

with names like "the kiss of death", an aptly named maneuver where the rider tosses their body forward and inverted with their head touching or just above the front fender. At least one attempt at a backflip has been made in competition, with top competitors like Travis Pastrana successfully landing in competition.

The sport is still young, and who knows what these riders will accomplish. The best riders will be continue to be talents like Pastrana, who can win Supercross and Freestyle competitions. How many top racers will be willing to risk competing in Freestyle and risk injuries which could keep them out of racing is yet to be seen. Surely, as Freestyle prize money grows, the attraction will, too.

Land & Ice Yachting

Land Sailing began hundreds of years ago in China when it was discovered that the power of the wind could be harnessed to make tasks like plowing and moving objects easier. Many historians believe the Chinese were the first to attempt to harness the wind for purposes of transportation, though there is reportedly evidence that the ancient Egyptians may have beaten them to it.

MODERN LAND YACHTS are capable of attaining speeds approaching 100 mph (160 kph)—the world record is 95.5 mph. Many modern land yachts are designed to swap out their wheels in the winter for ice blades. Ice yachts, with less friction to inhibit their speed, are now exceeding 150 mph (240 kph). Land and ice sailing designs are generally limited to modern three-wheel machines. There are some other approaches to land and ice sailing, such as skateboard-like systems employing either wheels or blades mounted to windsurfer rigs. These systems do not reach the velocities of their larger counterparts, but are none-the-less exciting and challenging to sail.

Land sailing on beaches is popular with enthusiasts, because wind blowing in off the sea, at right angles to the beach, is good for speed.

Finding the wind

Landsailing can be practiced on a broad range of surfaces. The dry lake beds of the U.S.A. are a favorite of landsailors globally.

Abandoned airfields are a great site for sailing, however they are more temperamental, since the asphalt direction and the wind direction don't always line up just right. Many land sailing enthusiasts enjoy sailing on beaches, which often offer a predictable breeze that is perpendicular to the required direction of travel, the preferred wind direction for beach sailing.

Ice yachts have a slightly easier time finding suitable ice to sail on. Their primary problem is finding lakes that are sizable enough to allow them to not only accelerate up to speed, but also to turn safely before coming ashore. There are techniques for spilling the air that allow the sailor to somewhat lower their terminal velocity, however, those techniques rely on the yacht not changing direction away from the wind's quadrant because doing so will change their apparent wind and accelerate their yacht.

Both land and ice yachts must deal with the concept of apparent wind when negotiating the terrain's limitations. Perhaps the easiest way to explain apparent wind would be to park your car so that the wind is hitting it at 90 degrees to the driver's door. If you were to take a reading on the direction of a wind blowing at 20 mph (32 kph) as it hit the door, the apparent wind would equal 20 mph at 90 degrees. If you then accelerated away to 20 mph, your apparent wind would increase to reflect the speed you were traveling versus the 20 mph wind hitting the side of your car. The angle of the apparent wind also changes to roughly 45 degrees forward of the driver's side. If you were to turn your car, both the angle and the speed of the apparent wind would change with you.

If understanding apparent wind seems complicated, it is. To drive a land or ice yacht at high speeds of 100+ mph, requires total driver control. A poor driver is a risk to other sailors and to themselves. Striking another vehicle traveling at 100 mph when you are also traveling at 100 mph is certainly not something any sane person would want to do. Focus and lightning reflexes mean the difference between a good day and a ride to the hospital.

Reflexes are not always good enough. Imagine sailing an ice boat at 150 mph (240 kph) and hitting a raised crack in the ice. This does happen, and the results are

Ice yachts, with less friction to inhibit their speed, can exceed 150 mph (240kph).

Driving land or ice yachts at high speed requires total driver control.

replacing these soft sails with hard adjustable wing designs that are lighter, more efficient, and allow for greater velocity. Wings are more easily "tuned" to either accelerate or decelerate the yachts, and the lift they generate to move the yacht can be positioned so as to effectively place the yacht into an "idle" mode.

The first recorded use of a land-sailing vehicle was around 1600 when Flemish Engineer Simon Stevin created a massive two-masted land yacht for beach travel. The yacht was capable of carrying a group of 28 passengers and could travel at speeds exceeding 20 mph.

Sailing the wild west

In the nineteenth century many attempts were made to create a sail-powered vehicle for transportation purposes. One of the more famous attempts was in the U.S., where the Baltimore and Ohio Railroad successfully used a special sailing railcar to transport, among others, the Russian Ambassador, who subsequently requested one for the Czar. Sailing railcars were most successful as workcars, and were reported to be capable of the speed of the fastest locomotives of the era. The sail railcars proved difficult to control and as unreliable as the wind, however, and soon vanished from the railroads.

rarely painless. Many ice sailors have had severe leg injuries and been killed in such instances. Land sailors have similar concerns, especially that of "capsizing" (tipping over) their craft. Unlike ice boats, which can slide through such an occasion, land yachts that capsize crash hard. Land yachts also run the risk of hitting unseen, or unforeseen objects at high speed, especially on dry lake beds.

Sails and wings

Modern land and ice boaters are constantly seeking new technologies to make their yachts both faster and safer. The use of composite materials together with modular construction techniques have helped to make the yachts lighter and better able to withstand impacts due to either capsize or striking debris. However, it is questionable if a remedy can be created for high speed collisions.

One of the most exciting high-tech modifications is the removal of the old wire "stayed" mast systems for hoisting the sails that power these yachts. New technology is

Later around the time of the California Gold Rush in 1849, many settlers and prospectors heading across the plains attached sails to Contessa Wagons, enabling them to travel further and faster than without the aid of wind power. These wagons did, however, have some substantial handling problems, as their extinction would indicate.

One thing is for sure, even if land and ice yachts are now only reserved for extreme sports enthusiasts, the opportunity to harness the wind in order to travel will always exist, and the urge to push the limits of performance will continue to redefine these exciting and dangerous sports.

Motocross

As off-road motorcycle riders have become more skilled, and as the equipment available from manufacturers has become consistently lighter and more powerful with an ever-increasing range of suspension travel, the physical boundaries of what can and can't be done on a motocross (motoX) bike are expanding. In the early days of off-road motorcycling, the thought that riders would someday leap 40 or 50 feet (12–15m) in the air, regularly, would have seemed absurd. However that is precisely the state of extreme motoX today. Extreme riding is not as new as today's riders would make it seem, though.

EXTREME RIDING is not as new as today's riders would make it seem, though. Hill climbs, trials riding (riders negotiate through a broad range of obstacles, requiring low speed, highly technical, balanced handling), and motoX racing have been part of motorcycle sport for years. In their day, many other riders pushed the limits of what had been done to that date. Daredevil rider Evel Knievel is a classic example of an early extreme pioneer, who also had a pretty good grasp of self-promotion.

The unique nature of the extreme sports movement today, is that extreme athletes have a multitude of other new sports and experiences to draw on. Extreme motoX is defined by more than just racing, although race series like the AMA Supercross Series have done much to showcase the talents of top extreme riders in the world. Extreme motoX riders push their machines in ways that are new and innovative and are drawing inspiration from other sports, such as skiing and snowboarding. Many of the top riders came from the ranks of BMX riders, and so a new freestyle orientation as to how a motoX bike is handled in the air is evident.

SuperX-over

AMA Supercross superstar Jeremy McGrath's rise through the motoX ranks is one example of taking BMX moves and bringing them to motoX. He is also a perfect example of what

Traditional motocross was simply off-road motorcycling, but the skills learned by the riders have had surprising results.

can be done when skill is coupled with newer technology and lighter motoX bikes. Along with others like Jeff Emig and Kevin Windham, he is redefining what can be done on a motoX bike. The Supercross riders are also impacting how the rest of the world views motoX. The brash and unique style of the AMA pros has been backed up by their ability to win races across the globe.

The best example of extreme motoX is the AMA Supercross Series. Here, the courses are designed to reward riders who can handle the most difficult of situations. The courses have many of the bumps and ruts of traditional motoX, but the obstacles and jumps are designed to maximize the height a rider can, and must, jump to win. Here is a brief description of a typical Supercross layout.

Supercross

The Start—as in traditional forms of motoX racing, the riders line up behind "the gate," a series of aluminum tubes that fall away from the riders when the start occurs. From here the riders go into Start Straight, where they tear out of the start and are forced into "the funnel," as the width of the straight decreases from 80 to 20 feet (24–6m) over the course of the 200–400-foot (60–120m)

section. This forces the riders to take a position in the "field" of riders before entering the first turn.

In Supercross, the First Turn is always a left—and it's crucial. As the riders leave the gate simultaneously, they are generally still positioning themselves as they come into the turn, so a few things happen. The front riders, especially the lead rider, have the advantage of getting through cleanly and extending their lead. But the First Turn forces riders in the main pack into one another, and a lot of crashes can occur. A rider can come through clean and get a shot at winning, or lose so much distance in a fall, that winning is virtually impossible.

The Obstacles—riders now weave their way through a series of turns that lead them over several obstacles (jumps), ranging from fairly easy to difficult and technically challenging. The jumps are designed to challenge a rider's ability to the fullest, create close racing, and maximize airtime. Jumps come in many sizes and are linked to create varying degrees of difficulty throughout he course. The jumps are categorized as:

● SINGLE JUMP – rider jumps 20–60 feet (6–18m) onto a flat landing
● DOUBLE JUMP – rider jumps off one obstacle and lands on the far side of the next, usually covering 20–70 feet of terrain

● TRIPLE JUMP – rider must get through three consecutive jumps and may choose to jump them as sets of two and one, or as a group of three (launching over an entire triple requires the rider to catch up to 25 feet (7.6m) of vertical air over a distance of 75 feet (23m) or more. Triples are real crowd pleasers)
● WHOOPS – a series of short and steep bumps across the entire width of the course that throw the rider about while crossing them.

The obstacles in Supercross give the riders enough time in the air to read *War And Peace*. Instead, they use the hang time to perform stylish trick maneuvers, many of which where created in BMX. Here are some of the most visually exciting:

● WHIP IT – moving the motorcycle from one side to the other in the air
● PANCAKE – pitching motorcycle and rider over to the side, as close to 90 degrees from vertical as possible
● CANCAN – taking one leg and bringing it across the motorcycle seat to the other side and back before landing
● NAC NAC – taking one leg off the back of the motorcycle and swinging backward to look at what's behind you while in the air. A move made famous by Jeremy McGrath

- **HELL CLICKER** – an insane move created by Kevin Windham where the rider lifts their feet and clicks their heels together in front of the motorcycle before landing
- **BAR HOP** – another insane move that's often practiced but unsuitable in a race where the rider takes their feet and places them on the handlebars before landing
- **SUPERMAN AIR** – another McGrath move where the rider holds on to the handlebars and lets the rest of their body to fly up away from the motorcycle while airborne.

The moves and obstacles in the Supercross Series are not natural, but many natural obstacles exist in areas that every rider can get to and play on. The machinery and technology of modern bikes has produced unprecedented opportunities to push the limits. Because the expanse of natural terrain is so broad, and so easily reached on a motoX bike, the only limitation of what can by ridden and how is defined by who's riding it.

One unfortunate aspect of motoX is that riders of all levels of ability and physical strength can get a motoX bike to go fast. As a result, every year riders are injured while performing stunts and tricks they are not prepared to handle, or over terrain they are unfamiliar with. The most important thing to remember for each motorcycle and motoX rider is that it's very easy to go fast and catch a lot of air, but it is not very easy to control and land the motorcycle. Take your time and learn at a reasonable pace, extreme riding requires years of practice, and excellent physical conditioning.

The Supercross series combines riding skills with new technology to produce spectacular riding action, indoors and out.

Mountain Biking

Charging down a hill at warp speed on a bike is a rush that most of us have enjoyed at some time. As bikes developed they headed down the path of tradition, and for a while, all a bike buyer could find was a road-racing-style bike or a cruiser. Road bikes were fine for speed and offered a broad range of gears. But road bikes offered little comfort and didn't take very well to rough surfaces. Cruisers were very comfortable, but heavy and not geared very well. All that changed in the early Eighties when a Japanese bike company by the name of Specialized purchased a unique bike made in Marin County, California, and took it home for a closer look.

Mountain bikes have opened up extreme terrain even for recreational riders and family outings.

THE MOUNTAIN BIKE can trace its roots back to when a small and unknown group of riders in Marin County, California first began riding stripped down and beefed up Schwinns on mountain roads just prior to WWII. One can only assume that the natural propensity of extreme oriented riders continued to pursue downhill riding until a few notable pioneers of the modern mountain bike began simultaneously experimenting and redefining the equipment they were riding. According to one of those pioneers, Gary Fischer, the early Schwinn "Ballooner" Cruiser bikes everyone was riding were so heavy that they were pushed, not ridden, uphill. Fischer is reported to have been the first to equip a

26

AP D´AIL

Downhill racers travel at speeds of
over 60 mph (97kph) requiring
state-of-the-art equipment to help
their aerodynamics.

Ballooner with multiple gears, an act that
made it easier to pedal uphill, but also added
25 lbs (11.35 kg) to their weight.

Specialized bikes

Racing provided inspiration for many of the
upgrades that are now taken for granted on
modern mountain bikes. Not suprisingly,
most of the advances in mountain biking took
place after the first official mountain bike

Even the salt flats of Death Valley in Nevada prove little obstacle to today's high-tech mountain bikes.

race took place on 21 October, 1976. The racers on the 2.1 mile (3.4km) course down Mt. Tamalpais could not possibly have known the biking revolution they were starting that day. The race was dubbed the Repack since the brakes required repacking after each heat due to the extreme pitch. Repack organizer Charlie Kelly was reported to have considered the race so extreme that he couldn't imagine many riders would get into it for very long.

In 1977, pioneer racer and bike builder Joe Breeze became the first to build a mountain bike from the stiffer and lighter chrome-moly materials used in road-racing bikes. To that he added the most lightweight and rugged components, giving birth to the first modern mountain bike. Five years later in 1983, Specialized would release its StumpJumper, the first mass-produced mountain bike made commercially available.

The release and overwhelming success of the StumpJumper fueled an explosion of demand for the new-style mountain bikes. Recreational riders had long been turned off by the dropped-style handlebars on all standard road bikes. The mountain bikes were so rugged and versatile that they could be ridden anywhere. Amazingly, sales of mountain bikes grew to surpass the sale of road bikes by 1986, and an entire global industry was born.

An early Schwinn "Ballooner" cruiser bike - arguably the first mountain bike.

The surge in sales demanded an entirely new set of accessories that were mountain bike specific. The balloon tires of the early Schwinns were replaced by "nobby, fat" tires that looked more like motocross tires than the skinny road tires on the bikes they quickly replaced. Road-style swept down handlebars were replaced by straight handlebars that were more comfortable. The saddles became more comfortable, too. A broader seating surface and padding, versus traditional road bike hard saddles, made the comfort package complete. The sum of fatter tires, straight handlebars, and softer saddles made converts out of riders who couldn't have cared less that the bikes they were buying could climb steep hills and fly down at high speed with great control.

Space-age materials

More accessories were added and new approaches to old needs created. Riders soon discovered that the addition of bar ends could allow them to shift their weight forward and upward in climbing situations. Bar ends are short sections of tubing, either straight or curved, that attach to the end of the handlebars at an angle of roughly 90 degrees. They were soon a requirement for racing, and many mountain bikers who didn't race got them as well. New clip in peddle systems were created with mountain bikers in mind, replacing the strapped in toe clip-

style retainers that didn't let a rider separate from their bike in a fall.

Innovation and competition continued to fuel the growth of mountain biking. Since Gary Fischer and Joe Breeze's first modifications in the Seventies, mountain bikes have been produced in a number of materials and frame styles, each focused on specific competitive needs. Materials now range from the chrome-moly in Joe Breeze's 1977 frame to aluminum, titanium, and space-age ceramic and composite materials.

The original one front sprocket (gear) and one rear sprocket single-gear set up gave way to three front and eight rear sprockets as gearing went from 1-speed to 3, to 10, to 15, to 18, to 21, to the highest currently available—24-speed gearing. Frame sets went from rigid to suspension forks with the introduction of the Rock Shock fork system. Soon, rear suspension was the rage, and full-suspension bikes continue to redefine performance on downhill and slalom courses. Now downhill racing bikes are created with full suspension in mind at the beginning of the design stage, not as an add-on feature. Suspension travel on some of the more radical designs exceeds 12 inches in the front rear, allowing for massive shock absorbtion at high speeds, increased tire contact at speed, and higher top end velocities. Downhill racers spent most of their time in "loose" tracking stances in early racing, with their rear tires drifting and their bikes constantly on the edge of control. Suspensions allow the riders to "carve" their turns now, using the suspension and their bodies to keep the tires locked into the terrain they are riding. New disciplines of mountain bike racing have evolved from mountain biking's popularity:

● CROSS COUNTRY RACING pits competitors against each other and the clock for best overall finish on a closed and gated course over grueling, technical terrain. Cross Country became an Olympic medal sport in 1996, replacing the dated and less popular road team time trial event.

● DOWNHILL RACING pits riders against the clock for best descent through a closed and gated course. The Eliminator race pits rider against rider for a best score of two runs. Speeds often exceed 60 mph (97 kph) and crashes are dramatic and painful.

● DUAL SLALOM RACING pits rider against rider on a closed gated course that requires the riders to execute a number of tight turns successfully on the way to the finish.

● OBSERVED TRIALS events require riders to complete a course consisting of obstacles and hazards. The riders must complete the course without "dabbing" (putting their feet down for balance). Riders are penalized by adding points for each dab. The rider with the least points wins.

● UPHILL RACING is a timed competition of sustained climbing where competitors finish at altitudes higher than where they started.

Take a hike

While all of these types of racing and styles of bikes have emerged during mountain biking's rapid evolution, the underlying allure of the kind of riding these bikes have allowed us to enjoy has not. The images and beauty of the outdoors are really why mountain biking has grown so rapidly. Mountain bikes have opened up an entire range of remote wilderness and landscapes that recreational trail hikers had never been able to get to so easily or quickly. Not suprisingly, many of the

Modern mountain bikes, like this Cannondale, utilize a whole range of innovations, like titanium, space-age ceramic and composite materials.

most popular mountain biking regions are established hiking areas.

With the emergence of bikes on hiking terrain came territorial issues of who should and shouldn't have access to the trails.

Not surprisingly hikers complained that mountain bikers weren't environmentally friendly enough to the trails, and were leaving trash and erosion problems behind them as they rode. Many of these complaints were justified, and organizations like the International Mountain Biking Association (IMBA) and the National Off Road Bicycle Association (NORBA) in the U.S. have worked hard to educate their members in order to decrease the impact mountain biking can have on the environment and on trails. Mountain bikes quickly reshaped the inner city messenger business, too. Urban dwellers and travelers can't help notice the volumes of bike messengers in virtually every city in the world. Modern cities are filled with hundreds of riders constantly riding through traffic, over curbs and stairs, and through parks in a quest for timely delivery. Not surprisingly, many of these riders are competing or aspiring professional mountain bike racers.

Mountainboarding

Mountainboarding is a newcomer to the world of extreme sports, although it can track its lineage to a few other more "established" extreme sports like snowboarding and mountain biking.

ESSENTIALLY, THE MOUNTAINBOARD creators developed a hybrid skateboard/snowboard that allows aspects of each sport to be used on terrain where neither can be practiced. Which isn't to say that skateboarders have not tried using fat tires on their skateboards so that they can ride on loose sand and gravel—they have.

Snowboarders also discovered that their boards can be made to double as sand surfers. However, until the mountainboard the only way to travel downhill at speed on a mountain road, over rocks, or gravel was on a mountain bike.

The name Mountainboard is a registered trademark of the Mountainboard company in Colorado Springs, Colorado. The company is owned by creators Patrick McConnell and Jason Lee, two Vail snowboarders who developed the board as a way to ride Vail during the summer as a cross-training tool for winter riding. The two soon discovered that the design rode so well that friends were buying as many as they could make, and a business was born from the idea.

Freestyle dirt

Another athlete on another continent created a similar vehicle at just about the same time. Australian surfer John Miln developed a three-wheeled board (the Mountainboard uses four) using a different steering setup a short while before the Vail snowboarders began. The Outback Mountainboard design uses two wheels in front to steer the rig and one at the back, and includes a brake.

Both systems are steered just like a skateboard, by leaning the board's deck in the required direction. On dirt and loose surfaces, the boards respond much like a snowboard. Riders can drive the rear of the board hard into the turn, "scrubbing" (slowing) their speed by getting the rear of the board slightly loose in the turn. On hard surfaces like pavement, they roll faster with fully-inflated tires, and slower on soft tires. This means that the rider stops just like a skateboarder—by getting off. They are said to be highly stable and controllable with practice.

While only a single model of the Outback is available, the rival Mountainboards are available in a variety of lengths, just like a snowboard. Shorter versions are for freestyle riding, while the longer ones offer better directional stability and are better suited to speed riding. Both take a range of tires, from slick pavement tires to knobby dirt tires.

Competition will determine the better board. With new competition from Mongoose, and continous improvements, such as new braking systems and lighter components, it appears that Mountainboard's four wheel version is where the market is headed.

Whichever wins consumers' hearts, there is no doubt that mountainboards are here to stay. Extreme athletes and enthusiasts will certainly take the opportunity to redefine what can be done on pavement or dirt, it only takes a few creative athletes to establish a new way to have fun doing it.

Mountainboards are a hybrid skateboard/snowboard that allows boarding on terrain which is not suitable for either.

The four-wheeled mountainboard is available in a variety of lengths: longer ones for speed, and shorter ones (as here) for freestyle riding.

Outdoor Climbing

Mountain climbing is as old as mankind. It has not always been a "sport," perhaps it was better classified as a survival skill. Now that we no longer require mountaineering skills to traverse the globe, those that still enjoy getting out into the mountains are clearly enthusiasts of the sport of mountain climbing.

Furthermore, while mountain climbing is the act of ascending a mountain under your own power, extreme mountain climbing is hardly a leisure activity.

CLIMBING MOUNTAINS covers two basic categories, technical and non-technical. The latter requires little more than sheer energy and knowledge of one's own limitations. No special equipment, just a good rugged and supportive pair of hiking shoes. Technical climbing requires the use of ropes and other specialized equipment to ascend the terrain to be climbed. The equipment is used so that, in the event of a fall, the climber is both protected from injury and securely fastened to the rock or ice.

Technical climbing can be broken into two components, ice and rock. Rock climbing involves scaling cliffs and boulders in situations that could prove hazardous or dangerous.

The most extreme rock climbers can scale the rock without the use of equipment beyond their shoes and some chalk to aid them in gripping the rock. These climbers "solo" their way up the faces of cliffs that are a match for many expert climbers even when they are using ropes or gear to keep them attached to the mountain in the event

of a fall. Because extreme solo climbers ascend without these aids, solo climbers are either very good, or very dead.

Ice climbing entails scaling cliffs and boulders that are entirely covered with ice and snow. Climbing ice requires an additional level of specialized equipment such as "crampons," the metal spikes which ice climbers attach to the bottom of their climbing shoes. In ice climbing, even the most proficient extreme climbers require the aid of equipment that allows them to grip the ice and snow without slipping.

Part of a team

Extreme climbers must be familiar with all of the technical gear, and must spend substantial time "on the rock" to successfully undertake those difficult climbs requiring highly specialized technique. The most difficult terrain demands a level of physical conditioning and mental toughness that few sports require. An extreme climber who has command of their body, mind, and surroundings can be considered relatively

safe in conditions that "normal" people would consider perilous.

Serious climbers do not "solo" (or climb alone). Climbing requires teamwork and a focus on not just personal safety, but the safety of the other climbers. Because climbers constantly rely on others to ensure their safety, it is important that everyone is aware of not only their personal limitations, but of those they are with as well.

Extreme mountain climbing ascents like Mount Everest or K2 are world famous not only for the climbers who have successfully reached their peaks, but also for the many

Isabelle Patissier of France solos her way up a sheer rock face in California, using chalk, shoes and tremendous climbing skills.

Frenchman Patrick Edlinger soloing up the Sugar Loaf mountain in Brazil, a challenge for even the best-equipped climbers.

who have failed or died in the process of the climb. To successfully climb peaks of this level of difficulty requires months of planning and a team of tremendous talent. Top expert abilities in both ice and rock climbing are essential requirements for those considering attempting an extreme mountain ascent. Each team of climbers that reaches the top can point to their climbing team members as well as dozens of support people at different stages of the climb, without whom the climb would have failed.

Danger categories

A complete knowledge of lifesaving and first-aid skills are also much needed assets in each team member. With the extreme altitude of these climbs, abrupt weather changes can strand an injured climber on the mountain for days before rescue is possible. Without sufficient first aid, a climber can die before outside assistance is made available. Because temperatures can quickly drop off the scale, advanced life-saving protective gear is also required, and must be available during the entire ascent and descent.

Most climbing is not, however, done in remote areas on massive peaks. It takes place within hours of major urban areas and towns around the globe. The fact that many climbing areas are accessible does not make them any less extreme. A simple categorization system has been created in every country to classify the difficulty of a climb. In France the system uses a series of numbers and letters; in England ascents are graded on difficulty and danger; in the U.S. climbers use what is termed the "Yosemite

Despite appearances, most climbing takes place within hours of major urban areas and towns around the globe.

Ice climbing is arguably the most extreme sport of all. It requires meticulous planning, the use of specialized equipment and complete reliance on other members of a team in the most dangerous circumstances.

One of the most famous climbers today is France's Catherine Destivelle. Here she demonstrates the sort of equipment required for a serious climbing expedition.

scale" to help explain the various levels of difficulty climbers can attempt. The Yosemite grading system uses the following structure for each climb:

● **CLASS I** – Hiking, where most any footwear is considered adequate.
● **CLASS II** – Proper footwear is required for rough terrain and the use of handholds may be needed in some portions of the ascent.
● **CLASS III** – "Scrambling" on hands and feet when use of the hands is required frequently. Ropes should be carried and available if needed.
● **CLASS IV** – Ropes and belays (the system of using ropes between climbers) must be used continuously for safety. Belay anchors may be necessary in some situations. (Class IV Climbs differ from Class III in that the terrain immediately adjacent to the climb is treacherous and a fall in that direction can be deadly.)
● **CLASS V** – Leader protection (anchors placed into the rock and used to secure the rope) required above the belayer.
● **CLASS VI** – Direct Aids must be used.

Climbs at Class V use a decimal system to detail the difficulty of the climb. The current top, which is of course open to opinion, is somewhere around a V.15. Once climbers get into Class VI, a scale of A0–A6 is used to detail the difficulty of this level.

● **A0** – Climb requires use of pre-existing aids (climber not required to place the assistance themselves).
● **A1** – Climb requires use of "chocks" (cam devices that anchor into openings in the rock) that are easy to place.
● **A2**– Climb requires the use of chocks that are difficult to place.
● **A3** – Climb requires the installation of a hook into the rock because chock placement is not possible.
● **A4** – Very "sketchy," aids used where the likelihood of the aid holding in the event of a fall is not high, very risky climbing.
● **A5** – Extremely sketchy.
● **A6** – So sketchy, the likelihood of A6 levels being climbable is debatable

Even the most basic technical climbing requires a fairly high level of specialist equipment.

Other terms used in climbing:

- **PITON** – metal blades or angles with an open eye at the blunt end which are driven into cracks in the rock to secure belays and leader protection.
- **CARABINER** – snaplinks of varying sizes and shapes used for connecting climbing rope with a piton, sling, or chock. These are made with either a "non-locking" spring gate closure or "locking" screw lock mechanism.
- **ROUTE** – a path up the rock where the ascent is made.
- **FLASH** – successfully climbing a to the top of a route without falling.
- **ON-SIGHT** – attempting to climb a route without any previous information or guidance.
- **WHIP OR AIRTIME** – a long fall (all long falls stop suddenly whether the rope holds or not).
- **OVERHANG** – a portion of the rock which stretches upward past the vertical.
- **ROOF** – a severe overhang requiring upside down climbing.
- **BUCKET** – a very good hold.
- **SMEAR** – holding on to the rock using friction from the climbers rubber footwear.
- **LUNGE** – climber throws him or herself at an out of reach hold (missing the hold means a fall).
- **BARNDOOR**—an out of balance climber swinging away from the rock.
- **FLAG**—using a free leg as a counterbalance to maintain control during a barndoor.

Mountain climbing is as old as mankind. Ascending a mountain under your own power holds a fascination for people from all walks of life.

Skateboarding

Without question, skateboarding is the embodiment of the outlaw extreme image. Somehow, skateboarding's unique style and underground culture have been difficult for older generations to understand or appreciate. Skateboarding is a sport that continues to redefine itself, pushing the limits of what can and can't be done physically, mentally—and yes, culturally.

NO ONE IS CERTAIN of the origins of skateboarding. Some have suggested the first skateboard was crafted by a bored California surfer seeking to polish his skills on a waveless afternoon. Others deny its West Coast origins, and state that the first skateboard was a simplified version of a child's toy, the push-scooter. Push-scooters were popular toys in the Fifties, made from dismantled roller skates nailed to a board with a crate attached as a balance aid. Remove the crate, and you have a skateboard.

New technology brought better wheels and trucks. These advances made new tricks possible and learning easier, and in the Seventies skateboarding boomed. By the end of the decade there were hundreds of skate parks, millions of skaters, and an industry was born.

Half-pipe and pool skateboarding were familiar images of early skateboarding. Names like Tony Alva, Jay Nelson, and Steve Caballero sprung up as heroes of this new sport.

Skateboarding's quick rise gave way to a decline in popularity due to inflated skate park admission fees and insurance issues. Many skate parks and manufacturers went bust. But hardcore skaters persevered, building backyard ramps and pushing streetstyle skating into the forefront of skateboarding's progression.

The springboard

In the early Eighties skateboarding began to organize itself in the U.S. Soon skaters in other countries began organizing too, and skateboarders worldwide began pushing their collective boundaries. Skaters like Tony Hawk and Steve Caballero pushed hard by setting the standards of achievement. Today, Tony Hawk continues to represent the pinnacle of skateboarding ability.

Skateboarding has impacted more than just its own world of sport. Skating can be linked directly to snowboarding, which has borrowed the half-pipe and many of skateboarding's moves and style. Skateboarding techniques can be seen in modern surfing style with its jumps and re-entry moves. Skateboarding is especially evident in the progression of inline skating, which has taken much of the style and culture of skateboarding and sought to make it

Sun and sea, skateboards and surf, but this is not Southern California; it is Newquay, Cornwall,

95

Street skaters seek out features of the urban landscape, like benches to jump, walls to ride, handrails and curbs to grind, and so on.

its own. Wakeboarding finds many of its roots in skateboarding. Street Luge is the most direct relative of skateboarding, and in fact got its start from folks lying down and going fast on skateboards before the term Street Luge was ever coined.

Street, vert and bowl

Skateboarding is now growing internationally, and faster than ever. Skating is one of only a handful of sports that has been embraced by young people globally. The top athletes in skateboarding are renowned worldwide within skateboarding circles. The sport is quickly moving out of the underground and into the mainstream, just as it did before its last peak. Yet, it is fair to point out that there are forces in place now that should serve to keep skateboarding alive and well for quite some time. Consider the number of sports skateboarding has fostered. Certainly all of the participants in those sports can respect skateboarding for what it truly is, a very physically and mentally challenging sport. Those who participate in these sports will naturally look to skateboarding for cross-training, and will encourage kids to get into it instead of discouraging skateboarding at all. Once this is accepted and once it's embraced by the mainstream, skaterphobics will be forced to relax their anti-skater rhetoric, back off, and let skaters do their thing.

Today's skateboarding can be categorized as either "street" or "vert." The object in both categories is for the skater to test the limits of

his ability and skill by trying to successfully land a trick and continue skating.

Street skating is the more technical style of skating. If you have ever seen a group of skaters trying the same trick over and over, they are practicing streetstyle skating tricks. Street skating is extremely difficult to master. Most of the tricks and moves are difficult to appreciate unless you happen to be a street skater or have ever tried street skating. Street tricks are performed on any, and every, available obstacle that looks like it can be ridden over or jumped. Park benches, hand rails, loading ramps, garbage cans, and even monuments are fair game.

Vert skating takes place in a half-pipe. The vert skating surface consists of two planes connected by a rounded transition. The name "vert" comes from the fact that the transition is from a horizontal plane to a vertical plane. Skaters drop down into the transition from the vertical plane, across the horizontal plane, back up the opposing transition to the opposing vertical plane. Or put quite simply, a half-pipe resembles a big "U" and the skaters go up and down inside of it.

Pools have been a big draw for skaters since the skateboarding began. Generally, any pool left empty and accessible (by virtually any means) is fair game for skating. With a wide variety of shapes, transitions, and depths, pools are extremely challenging to skate. Pool skating has influenced the construction and design of bowls specifically for skating. Bowls, constructed of either concrete or wood, generally pay homage to pools through choice of shape, the use of pool coping instead of typical metal coping found on most vert and mini ramps, and other common features.

Half-pipes are measured by overall width, the radius of the transition, the height of the vertical plane, or vert, and the length of the horizontal plane, or flat. A competition half-pipe is commonly around 32 feet wide (9.75m) with a 10 foot (3m) transition radius, 12–18 inches (30–46cm) of vert, and 16 feet (5m) of flat.

One component critical to making a half-pipe ridable is what is called the "coping." This is usually a 2.5 inch (6.35cm) diameter pipe that sits on the top of the vert plane. The

Steve Caballero performs a tweaked backside air.

A skater airs out of a concrete bowl.

coping sticks out beyond the edge around 0.25–0.375 inches (6–10mm) and acts as a physical and audible cue, telling the skater he's crossed the top of the half-pipe. The coping also acts to deflect the skateboard back at the skater, allowing enhanced control of the board in the air. Too much coping makes the ramp unridable, too little, makes it extremely difficult to ride. Finally, the coping acts as the surface on which the skater can perform a number of tricks from a "grind" to a "blunt."

All skateboards are essentially the same and share the same basic components. Each skateboard has a deck which is the platform the skater stands on. Decks have been made of fiberglass and plastic, but are almost always made of wood these days.

Each board has a front, or "tip," and a back, or "tail." The length of the tip and tail is determined by the distance from the trucks to the end of the board. The sides of the deck are called rails. The front rail is on the toe side, while the back rail is on the heel side.

Stunt and cruiser

Mounted to every deck is a set of "trucks." Trucks are the steering and axle assemblies on which two wheels are mounted. Trucks are available in a variety of widths. Skateboards all have four wheels, two on the front trucks, two on the rear trucks. Wheels are available in a wide array of widths and diameters, and also in different compounds. Compounds vary by their hardness and traction. Generally, harder wheels offer less traction than softer wheels. Each skater has their own preference when it comes to wheel size and compound.

There are two basic types of skateboards: stunt boards and cruiser boards. Stunt boards are designed to be agile and easy to throw around when performing tricks. Stunt boards are either "old school" or "new school" designs and are used to skate street and vert. Old school boards are wide with longer, wider tails than tips. New school boards are narrower and with symmetrically shaped tips and tails, however their tips are longer than their tails. Old school boards generally use wider trucks than new school boards. Cruiser boards are a lot longer than stunt boards, and tend to use wide trucks for added stability and tracking at speed.

There are two ways to stand on a skateboard. A "regular foot" stance means that the skater places his left foot on the front end of the board. A "goofy foot" means that the skater places his right foot on the front end of the board.

Skateboarders have created a variety of names for the tricks they do. Many times skaters use a mixture of terms to name tricks. These are some of the more frequently used terms:

- FRONTSIDE TRICK – skater turns so that his heels are facing the inside of the turn
- BACKSIDE TRICK – skater turns so that his toes are facing the inside of the turn
- KICK FLIP – skater spins the board around the axis running from the tip to the tail of the board with his toe by kicking his front foot in a backward motion
- HEEL FLIP – skater spins the board around the axis running from the tip to the tail of the board with his heel by kicking his front foot in a forward motion
- FRONTSIDE AIR – skater jumps frontside and grabs the front rail with his back hand
- SLOB – skater jumps frontside and grabs the front rail with his front hand
- STALE FISH – skater jumps frontside and grabs the back rail with his back hand
- LEAN AIR – skater jumps frontside and grabs the back rail with his front hand

- BACKSIDE AIR – skater jumps backside and grabs the back rail with his front hand
- MUTE – skater jumps backside and grabs the front rail with his front hand
- INDY AIR – skater jumps backside and grabs the front rail with his back hand
- TAIL GRAB – skater jumps and grabs tail with front or back hand
- NOSE GRAB – skater jumps and grabs the tip with front or back hand
- INVERT – skater jumps and sets one hand down and balances while upside down holding the board with the other hand
- BLUNT – skater lands the tail on the coping or object in front of both trucks
- SHUVIT – skater jumps and spins the board in 180-degree increments without spinning his body
- SWITCH STANCE – skater lands on the board and rides in the opposite stance, ie. goofy to regular foot
- 540 – skater jumps and spins 540 degrees with the board
- MCTWIST – a 540 with an inverted twist
- CAB – named after Steve Caballero who invented it, skater spins 360 degrees without grabbing the board
- HALF CAB – skater spins 180 degrees without grabbing the board.

Skateboarding action at the Rip Curl Board Masters, Newquay, Cornwall, August 2001

99

Snowboarding

All forms of sport need an element of revitalization or they risk becoming commonplace. Skiing has been a part of life for anyone living near snow-covered or mountainous regions of the globe. With the advent of cheap international air travel, skiing as a sport for the masses progressed until it reached saturation point—interest and participation waned. And then the surfer-skateboarder axis saw snow glinting on distant hills...

IN 1965 a Michigan industrial gases engineer began toying with a design that would wind up saving the the entire ski industry some 25 years later. Sherman Poppen noticed his daughter attempting to stand up on her sled while sliding on the neighborhood hill. This inspired him to go to his garage, where he took a pair of children's skis and screwed them together with dowels, which he described as acting like "foot stops." His daughter Wendy took the "sled" to the hill and rode it. When the other kids saw what her dad had created, they all wanted him to build one for them, too. He did, and they were an instant hit.

Poppen's wife mixed the words surfer and snow together to coin the name "Snurfer," and a product was born. Poppen manufactured Snurfers and distributed them through sporting goods and toy stores, and over the next ten years sold millions. It was the Snurfer that would inspire snowboarding

Siegfried Grabner of Austria is one of the world's most accomplished snowboarders.

Without the culture associated with skiing, snowboarding is free to develop in its own sweet way.

Above: Rhys Crabtree is parallel to the snow in Chamonix, France.

Below: Ed Leigh looks as if he is snowboarding off the mountain at Lofoten, Norway.

pioneers like Jake Burton Carpenter to develop and manufacture designs that led to the modern snowboard in use by millions of riders today.

One board good...

Early converts to snowboard riding shared a passion that inspired others to give snowboarding a try. The feeling of riding a snowboard has been described many different ways, but perhaps the best term is "soulful." Just as skateboarding and surfing have a zen-like quality to them, snowboarding, especially in deep, fresh, powder, delivers a sensation that is about as close to pure harmony as any extreme sport offers. Anyone who has experienced snowboarding has a clear understanding of why so many young and older people are converting from skiing to snowboarding, and why so many swear they will never return to riding two boards.

Since its start, snowboarding has progressed from simple boards crudely constructed from wood with metal fins attached—meant as a steering aid—to many of the high-tech wood and foam-core construction methods that ski manufacturers have been refining for years. The result is that today's snowboards are so stable and

Part of the appeal of snowboarding is its simplicity and its addictivness.

Silhouetted against the moon, a snowboarder takes to the air.

controllable that many outperform skis in a variety of conditions, especially soft snow and "crude," when snow is chopped up and inconsistent in texture and density.

Early designs used clumsy footstraps that offered little control. Today, binding systems fall into two basic categories: hard boot and soft boot. Hard boot systems are the least popular, yet are necessary equipment for those racing gates. The hard boot eliminates the feel that riders seek, and dramatically alter the techniques needed for performance. Soft boot systems use rigid metal or composite frames mounted directly to the board, which utilize straps to retain the rider's boots in place. Soft boots allow the rider to connect to the board using either metal or composite bindings, using straps or

boot sole mounted step in systems. Soft boots provide the best fit and feel in all conditions, especially soft snow and powder.

The cultural revolution

Snowboarding was reviled for years by skiers and the ski industry. Early on, most mountains would not allow snowboards on their lift systems or their slopes.

These confrontations were when snowboarders, who justly felt they had a right to be on the hill, responded strongly and aggressively in their own defense. More than a few verbal and physical brawls resulted, enhancing skiers' perception that all snowboarders were bad news.

These cultural boundaries are now breaking down as skiers begin to appreciate

Like a giant sidewinder, a snowboarder leaves a trail in fresh snow.

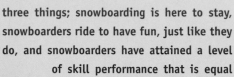

The growing popularity of the sport has forced people to sit up and take notice.

Snowboarder James Kemp (top right) is almost lost in the breathtaking scenery at Alpine Meadow, Tahoe, California.

three things; snowboarding is here to stay, snowboarders ride to have fun, just like they do, and snowboarders have attained a level of skill performance that is equal to or higher than skiing in many ways.

Yet, many skiers still believe it is their God-given right to verbally assault snowboarders without any real justification.

However, it is generally skiers possessing little skill or confidence who choose to act confrontationally, since they lack the understanding or respect necessary to appreciate what snowboarders can do on the mountain.

Snowboarding has brought a new look to the hills, with its "fun park" concepts. These specially created areas have "hits" (jumps) and obstacles like rails, tables, and even buried cars and buses, that the riders enjoy jumping over and sliding across. Skiers have appreciated these additions because it meant snowboarders kept more to themselves. Snowboarders appreciate the parks because they offer a challenging alternative to some of the more mundane terrain that skiers covet.

Another major impact on snowboarding has been the creation of long half-pipes. Half-pipe riding is now a speciality of many top pro snowboarders, with many moves directly adapted from skateboarding. The half-pipe gives snowboarders an opportunity to rhythmically link a number of airborne trick maneuvers as they descend the slope on which the half-pipe is constructed. They attract masses of riders to mountains that build them, and many riders prefer to climb up the side of the pipe for each ride rather than use the available chair lift system.

Find that "air"

Though discouraged by some snowboarding pioneers like Jake Burton Carpenter when they were introduced at the first World Snowboarding Championships in 1983, half-pipe freestyle competitions are major events in most of today's top competitions.

Another fun and exciting snowboarding competition is called "boardercross," because the courses constructed for the races resemble motocross courses. There are a series of right- and left-hand turns on embankments called "burms" that let riders maximize their speed. Between the burms are jumps and bumps to keep the riders on the edge of control and add to the difficulty. Boardercross offers a sharp contrast to skiing's traditional gate racing. The boardercross format pits as many six racers

against one and other simultaneously, each fighting the other for position into the turns and, of course, at the finish line.

"Big air" contests make an exciting spectacle for spectators. The jumps are specially built and riders speed into them for style and dramatic air. Riders are scored on their performance by a panel of judges.

The most dangerous event is undoubtedly the steep "extreme" riding contests, generally held on slopes exceeding 50 degrees in pitch. Falling almost certainly means losing the event, but it can also end in

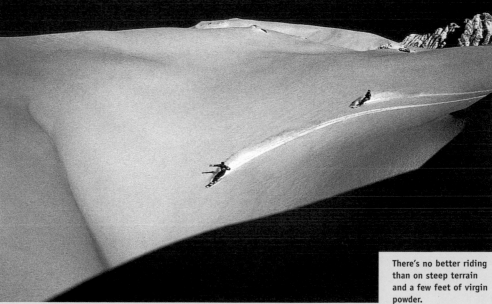

There's no better riding than on steep terrain and a few feet of virgin powder.

108

serious injury. Given the steepness of the angle, a rider may actually accelerate during a fall, tumbling uncontrollably past rock outcrops and possibly over large cliffs. Steep and extreme riding requires the highest levels of technical and physical skill to get top to bottom while seeking extra points for jumping over and off obstacles.

Not everyone enjoys communal activities on packed slopes. Many snowboarders prefer trekking into mountainous backcountry on snowshoes to find untouched powder. Climbing adds to the physical challenge of riding the backcountry, while pleasure and satisfaction may be gained from experiencing the mountain in the absence of other people. For those with the wherewithal and a preference for less initial effort, using a helicopter or snowcat and being dropped into the terrain to be ridden is an option. On clear days helicopters get you up fast and high, free to enjoy tens of thousands of vertical feet during the course of a day. Snowcats take a bit longer, but have the advantage of being able to deliver in nearly all weathers. Remember, the powder is at its best when it's snowing hard.

Soon, the number of snowboards is expected to exceed that of skis. Younger and younger kids are drawn to snowboarding, so the growth should continue. The popularity of snowboarding lies in its alternative to skiing, and that it offers a winter crossover for surfers and skateboarders seeking fun in the snow. Snowboarding continues to attract new riders because the technology has made it easier to learn, and the feeling is addictive. Even if the terrain is not extreme, a snowboard is what it's best to be on.

Wind snowboarding

Once down at the bottom of the mountain, what do you do next? It wasn't long before boarders realized that adding a windsurfing-style sailing rig to their board would allow them to sail back up the slopes, without needing a lift or hike. All they needed was wind direction from the side or directly up the slope of the terrain. Directly uphill is preferable, as it has the added advantage of making it easy to sail down again, but a side wind is good for speed.

Snowboarders who are boardsailors and boardsailors who are snowboarders, can easily find enough stuff to put together a wind snowboard. In fact, any long snowboard will do the trick. Snowboard sailing doesn't require sails as large as boardsailing, because small sails and short booms are the most controllable, particularly on hard-packed snow.

The addition of foot straps adds to the stability of the rider, and a helmet is vital to avoid very painful contact with the snowy surface of the ground at high speed. Sailors also have to be aware of obstacles hidden beneath the surface of the snow.

Though still in its infancy, wind snow-boarding is a natural extension of board-sailing, that will grow modestly during the next few years. The main obstacle to its growth is that wind snowboard sailors need to be boardsailing experts before they start. It would be foolish to attempt to learn wind snowboard skills first, because mistakes are always painful and often dangerous, whereas it is still painful but less dangerous to be

slammed in the water when learning.

The progress of the sport remains to be seen. Will boards be used to cover long distances? Will new designs be created especially for this new sport? Will drift jumping on wind snowboards become the new winter rage? Only time will tell. But if the history of extreme sports tells us anything, it tells us that these extreme athletes will push their boards and the technology to new lmits. The next decade of wind-powered snowboarding should prove to be quite interesting.

Top British snowboarder James Kemp during an international competition at Squaw, Tahoe, California, in May 2001.

Snowshoeing appeals to many because it is an extreme sport that requires minimal equipment and, if administered responsibly, will not have a harmful effect on the environment.

Snowshoeing

Like some of the other extreme sports, snowshoeing got its start not as a sport but as a means of survival. Its roots go back some 6,000 years, when people who lived in predominantly snowbound regions needed to augment their footwear to get through untracked regions. In fact, snowshoes are directly linked to the spread of mankind into regions around the globe where heavy snowfall is a part of life.

AS LONG AS there have been snowshoes, snowshoeing has drawn users out for pleasure treks in addition to using them for survival. Therefore, it is difficult to pinpoint exactly when snowshoeing made the transition from survival skill to sport. Certainly, in the early twentieth century more and more people began getting outdoors for social trekking in the colder climate areas. Snowshoeing was widely used in both WWI and WWII as troops sought to secure regions in the Alps and other areas covered by snowfall. One of the more famous uses of snowshoes occurred when Admiral Byrd relied on them to get to the South Pole—certainly an extreme spot. Snowshoeing as sport has grown out of the outdoor, extreme sports movement. Snowshoes were long overlooked by other extreme athletes until it was realized that they are an effective method of transportation—now, snowshoes are required equipment in the snowy back country. In difficult and isolated terrain, snowshoes can deliver extreme skiers and snowboarders to locations that without the aid of helicopters or snowmobiles they would have otherwise only dreamt about. In fact, snowshoes help to keep the natural spirit of these sports from being overwhelmed by machines.

Breaking the trail

Snowshoe racing was an outgrowth of the Eighties fitness craze, and today hundreds of races are held around the globe each year. Racing has encouraged the participation of many who would have otherwise never snowshoed, and has broadened the appeal to include folks who would just like to get out and enjoy nature rather than being bound by the path of a snowplow.

Snowshoes are designed to be light and provide floatation in heavy and light snow. Getting out and traveling in fresh or untracked snow requires the lead snowshoer to "break trail." This is the most difficult aspect to snowshoeing, and can require as much as ten times the energy than "sucking trail," or following in someone else's snowsteps. This is because the person breaking trail must take strides that not only move them forward, but also pack and compress the snow beneath their shoes.

Getting cold-prepared

Snowshoes are also designed to ascend steep and icy terrain. They have "claws" on the bottom that stick down into the snow to provide additional bite for better traction. Ascending is when they are most frequently used by extreme mountaineers, skiers, and snowboarders.

Snowshoeing is growing rapidly because it involves getting away into remote, peaceful, and natural settings. The fact that the settings can produce fatigue, dehydration, and hypothermia should not be overlooked by anyone considering trying snowshoeing. However, with the right clothing and protective gear, snowshoeing is a great extreme sport that can be enjoyed by a wide range of enthusiasts.

Speed Biking

Traveling down a snow-covered 60-degree slope at an excess of 125 mph (200 kph) on a skis is without question extreme. In fact, the 150 mph (240 kph) record for speed skiing was recently established. Is there any doubt that riding a mountain bike down that very same slope and seeking to achieve that very same speed is extreme too?

OVER THE PAST FEW YEARS, downhill mountain bike racers have been pushing the limits of speed on specially outfitted mountain bikes, and have already broken the 125 mph threshold. The bikes are fitted with special aerodynamic fairings and tires modified with large spikes to grip the snow and ice-covered surface as they accelerate to maximum velocity before racing through a speed-trap zone (a timed distance that determines the official speed established by the rider).

Speed bikes are wind tunnel-tested to improve aerodynamics before racing. Both rider and bike are outfitted to slice through the wind, and the resulting forms are thin and offer little resistance. The bikes are both

Speed bikes are windtunnel tested to ensure that they slice through the wind with minimum resistance. Spiked tires allow the bike to grip the snow and ice surfaces on which they race.

suspended and unsuspended, and are raced in stock class and modified class. The suspension designs are stiffer than what you'd expect to get off the shelf and give the rider a margin of error at speed that a rigid frame cannot, allowing for higher terminal velocities.

The current world record for speed biking is held by Frenchman Eric Baron, who was

Eric Baron (left), is the current world record holder for speed biking. He has achieved speeds in excess of 130 mph (200kph).

traveling at exactly 200 kph when he went through the speed trap. Considering the world record for speed skiing is now 60+ kph (150 mph) above that, we can expect to see far higher speeds as the technology of speed biking improves.

Speed biking is still relatively new as a sport, so it is safe to expect that the records established today will be broken and reestablished soon. Many world class mountain bike downhill racers and speed skiing racers crossing over to speed bikes will be working hard to determine the modifications needed for both equipment and training to make new records possible. The next few years should be very interesting.

Speed Skiing

Skiing in its own right is a pretty extreme sport, and has been for years. One skiing discipline that is as amazing as it is extreme is speed skiing. Imagine screaming down a mountain at 150 mph (240 kph) on skis. That is exactly what current World Record holder and 1992 Olympic Bronze medalist Jeff Hamilton of Truckee, California did in 1995 at Vars, France, becoming the first skier to break the 150 mph barrier, and the fastest non-motorized human on the planet.

Speed skiers' helmets give them the appearance of aliens from another planet.

CONSIDER THE FORCES at play when traveling at 150 mph. The skier is literally skiing faster than a sky diver in freefall. The skis are no longer even touching the ground at that speed. Instead they are riding on a cushion of air. Even the slightest error in judgment or form at that speed can be deadly.

What if a skier was to fall at speed? If they were fortunate enough not to break anything (legs, arms, etc.), it is unlikely they would avoid the residual burns that a high speed fall on snow leave behind. The suits the skiers wear, while great at reducing drag, are not good at preventing tremendous heat build up from the friction of the snow during a fall. The result is often severe burns that can take months to heal. Former World Champion Franz Weber was reported to have spent well over one year healing from burns suffered during a high speed fall.

Shaped like a plane

Clearly, if an athlete wishes to speed ski, they must be a top expert skier and in tremendous physical condition. The forces on the skier's body during acceleration and at terminal velocity are tremendous. Wind tunnel training is one key to finding a low-drag stance. It is expensive, but it allows top competitors to find a position through low-risk testing in a controlled environment. However, the fact remains that at some point, the skier will be asked to point their skis down a 2-mile (3.2km), 60-degree slope in an effort to establish a new record, or at least beat their competition. If that isn't enough, at the bottom of that run, when their muscles are at their most taxed, they will need to find the energy to stop.

Speed skiers employ many specialized pieces of equipment when performing their sport. First, their head protection is a strange looking helmet that is designed to fit flush with their upper body, minimizing any speed-robbing drag. Their poles are special aerodynamically-shaped units, complementing their low-drag theme. Even the boots are modified for reduced drag, and their lower legs are smoothed by the addition of wing-like pants to further eliminate drag. Of course, all of these aero-additions don't mean squat if the skier can't hold a decent position during their run. That is where physical conditioning and endurance, preparation and mental toughness differentiate first from last.

Speed skiing competitions are held throughout Europe, but mostly in France, where they are major events. In North America, there are no areas that are accessible for speed skiing, and insurance and tort law problems make attempting events difficult, so the sport is widely overlooked. Speed skiing is rapidly gaining exposure and popularity globally, as the demand for more and varied extreme sport competitions grows.

115

While popular in Europe and included in the Winter Olympics (as here in Lillehammer, Norway 1994), insurance and legal problems have kept the sport limited in North America.

Steep Skiing

For years skiing has symbolized the carefree pursuit of sport in paradise-like winter settings around the world. Since the first skier rode downhill somewhere in Scandinavia, skiing has drawn free-spirited athletes to the mountains. But enjoyment of the sport became for many only a lifestyle statement, and the thrill of challenging terrain and conditions seemed to dwindle. Now a new generation of extreme athletes are redefining the meaning of downhill skiing.

Skiing backcountry powder, or resort groomed terrain, skiing is a blast.

Backcountry skiing is ever more possible with the addition of snowcat and helicopter access.

Scottie Ewing skis with snowshoes, climbing gear and avalanche safety equipment.

SKI RESORTS HAVE TAMED SKIING. Snowcats, towed terrain-grooming equipment, gentle pistes, vista spots, posh resort restaurants—not long ago skiing was a very different pursuit of sport and challenge, and the relaxation came from winning a personal test of ability. Early skis were more like coasting snowshoes, used for survival and hunting (and undoubtedly fun as well). Then some nordic skiers (on nordic skis only the toe of the skier's boot is attached to the ski), tiring of fighting their gear on difficult descents, started fixing their heels down to create what would become known as alpine skiing. That in turn led to the first ski lifts, since the whole idea of alpine skiing is to ride down, not up.

Opening up the slope

Steep descents in the early days of alpine skiing required many of the mountaineering skills that today's top extreme skiers continue to use. Snowshoes, climbing gear, and avalanche safety equipment remain standard gear, with the obvious addition of helicopter and snowcat access to remote regions. These new transportation options have expanded the amount of terrain available for skiing, as well as the difficulty of the terrain that can be skied. Slopes of 60 degrees or more are not uncommon for the very best to ski successfully.

Ski, boot, and binding technology has improved dramatically over the years, reducing the number of injuries and adding valuable control to skiers who seek out steep

The world's top steep skiiers face slopes of over 60 degrees.

terrain. Some resorts even invite skiers to sample lift-served steep skiing as the popularity of extreme skiing has grown.

Although alpine skis would seem the most appropriate, it's not necessarily so. Alpine touring binding lets skiers free their heels for limited movement, giving them a way to climb with their equipment. But nordic equipment has also been refined, and now gives free-heeled telemark skiers the kind of added control that was not available even in the early days of alpine technology. As a result, many different athletes ski extreme terrain on a broad range of skiing equipment.

Exotic locations

Extreme skiing has been widely popularized by film makers, like Warren Miller and Greg Stump, whose movies are favorites worldwide. As skiers became more familiar with the types of terrain that were skiable, extreme steep skiing grew among those who saw skiing as a personal challenge. With the glamorization of steep skiing and the top experts who are featured in these films, more and more skiers are pushing it to "go big."

Going big means skiing the steepest terrain, dropping off large cliffs, and flying through the air. With top skiers this usually means

"Going big" on the Trash Chutes, Whitewater, British Columbia.

a controlled landing. With skiers who seek to emulate the top extreme skiers, but haven't yet developed the skills, this means pain. Every year, more and more extreme wannabees are getting themselves hurt, or even killed, attempting terrain and air that is too technical for their abilities. The lesson here is that to ski the most difficult terrain an athlete must be able to ski under

control no matter how steep the pitch or how big the air. Even the best still get injured...and occasionally killed.

The European Alps, the North American Rockies, the South American Andes, and the Southern Alps of New Zealand all attract skiers from around the world for steep skiing adventures each year, and an entire industry has sprung up around providing access to

120

Steep skiiers must be able to control their skis no matter how steep the pitch or how big the air. Failure can be disastrous.

There are few things in life that can match the feeling of charging down a steep powder run.

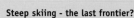

Steep skiing - the last frontier?

steep terrain. Each year thousands of skiers, and now snowboarders, travel to remote mountain peaks for a few thousand vertical feet of untracked terrain, an extreme skier's dream. There are very few things in life that can match the feeling of charging down a steep powder run.

The last frontier

A series of international events focusing on steep-terrain skiing have popped up over the past few years in each of these regions, with the World Championships held each year in Valdez, Alaska. These events are a fantastic showcase for not only the best extreme terrain skiers in the world, but also for some of the most beautiful places in the world. The interest in the events is exploding throughout the skiing world and beyond both because of the challenge and the scenery these events offer.

Extreme skiing is the last frontier of modern skiing, it fills the void for skiers who no longer find skiing in groomed terrain to be as exciting as it was. As skiing extreme regions becomes more and more popular, expect to find a lot more folks heading to the steeper challenges of technical terrain, and expect to see the future of skiing defined by extreme skiers.

Street Luge

The ice luge is an Olympic sport with which most of the world is familiar, and which few would deny is extreme. Enter the pavement version of the sport, street luge. While street lugers don't have specially-constructed tracks for their use, they do find steep and winding roads to roar down at speeds exceeding 70 mph (113 kph).

LIKE ICE LUGE, which can trace its roots to traditional sledding pushed to the limit, street luge is an extension of another form of downhill pavement travel...skateboarding. In fact, skateboarders have traveled downhill on their boards at speed, both lying down on their backs like a street luge, on their stomachs, and standing up.

The street luge is an evolution of the traditional skateboard design. The wheels and trucks (the combined axle and steering mechanism) used by skateboards and street luges are pretty much the same, though luges tend to have wider axles than skateboards. The decks used by skateboarders (the board part of a skateboard) are replaced by stiffer metal and composite-frame systems that allow the street luge to be made longer and track better than a skateboard.

Looking for velocity

Decks on street luges must be stiffer because as the speed of the boards increase, the stresses placed on the decks increase to the point that a deck that is not stiff enough will begin to move, allowing the wheels to wobble. The "high speed wobbles" are a big factor in limiting terminal velocity, not only in skateboards, but also inline skates, partly because the wheels do not have enough diameter or mass to stabilize themselves through centripetal force.

Once the luge deck is acceptable, the most important equipment to consider is, of course, the wheels themselves. At the speeds

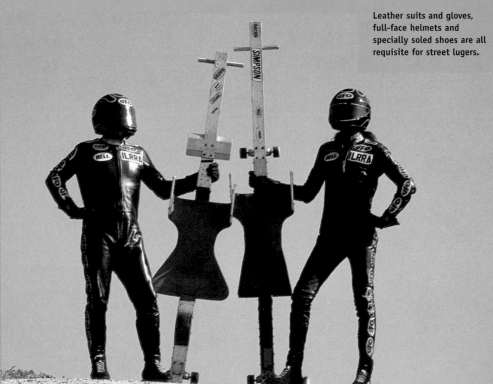

Leather suits and gloves, full-face helmets and specially soled shoes are all requisite for street lugers.

On the road in Los Angeles, California.

that street luges can travel, the bearings used to keep the wheels attached to the axles must work very hard, spinning almost as quickly as the wheels themselves. The slightest bit of friction within the bearing can "toast" a wheel, creating enough heat to melt the wheel where it contacts the bearing, and bringing a run to a quick stop. Therefore, street lugers pay particularly close attention to the details of cleaning and preparing their wheels before they start. Even so, dirt and dust particles can work their way into a bearing while the luger is moving, and the result can be the same.

Because lugers are traveling at high speeds on pavement, they must wear protective gear while riding. Most make use of the leathers worn by motorcycle riders and racers, which are generally expected to take all the abuse the luger's skin would suffer in the event of a fall. Leather gloves are also worn and a full-face helmet is necessary.

Pavement rockets

The final, and perhaps most important, piece of street luge equipment is the rider's footwear. The shoes are used as brakes, at which point they are exposed to the same kind of extreme heat as the wheels and bearings. Obviously, not just any shoe will work. Lugers use modified sneakers or boots to stop themselves. Typically, a section is

removed from an automobile tire and fixed to the shoes' soles, giving them grippy rubber capable of stopping a car without melting, never mind a luge.

Street luging got its unofficial start in the foothills of Southern California, where groups of riders first began flying down the steep, smooth, and winding roads for thrills. They soon began organizing races, and the sport was born. Street luging is still relatively new, and so we can expect a variety of improvements in the technology and speed of these pavement rockets as the sport develops. Who knows, someday maybe we'll even see specialty tracks like the ones used in ice luge.

Water
Sports

Water nourishes, and brings death. We are not naturally built to survive in it, but we are drawn to its many possibilities for extreme sports.

FURTHER INFORMATION

BIBLIOGRAPHY

- *Personal Watercraft*, Jack C. Harris, Edited by Michael E. Goodman, Crestwood House, Mankato, Minnesota, 1988
- *All Action Kayaking*, Alan Fox, Lerner Publications Company, Minneapolis, Minnesota, 1993
- *A Trailside Series Guide: Kayaking*, Steven M. Krauzer, W. W. Norton & Co., New York, London, 1995
- *British Ocean Racing*, Douglas Phillips-Birt, Adlard Coles Ltd., 1960
- *Great Yacht Races*, Bob Fisher, Stewart, Tabori & Chang Publishers, New York, 1984
- *Surfing The Ultimate Pleasure*, Leonard Lueras, Workman Publishing, New York, 1984
- *Great Surfing*, Edited by John Severson, Doubleday & Co., Inc., Garden City, New York, 1967
- *The Complete Guide to Windsurfing*, Jeremy Evans, Facts on File Publications, New York, NY, 1983

ASSOCIATIONS & CLUBS

AIR CHAIR
- Water Skier's Web - Air Chair
  http://waterski.net/ac/index.html

BOARDSAILING
- U.S. Windsurfing Association
  PO Box 978, Hood River, OR 97031
  Tel: (001) 503 386 8708
  uswa@aol.com
- World Boardsailing Association
  Feldafinger Platz 2,
  München 71 D-8000
  Germany
  Tel: (0049) 89/781074
- *Body Boarding* (magazine)
  PO Box 3010
  San Clemente, CA 92672
  Tel: (001) 714 492 7873
- *Windsurfing Magazine*
  330 W. Canton
  Winter Park, FL 32789
  Tel: (001) 407 628 4802
- Windsurfing Glossary
  http://allserv.rug.ac.be/
  wdobbel/windserf/lexicom.html

JET SKIING
- International Jet Ski Boating Association
  1239 E, Warner Ave
  Santa Ana, CA 92705
  Tel: (001) 714 751 4277 or 714 751 8418

KAYAKING
- Trade Association of Sea Kayaking
  12455 N. Wauwatosa Rd.,
  Mequon, WI 53097
  Tel: (001) 414 242 5228
- American Canoe Association
  7432 Alban Station Blvd, Suite B-226
  Springfield, VA 22150
  Tel: (001) 703 451 0141
- *Canoe and Kayak Magazine*
  PO Box 3146,
  Kirkland, WA 98083
  Tel: (001) 206 827 6363

KITEBOARDING
- www.kiteworld.net
- www.kiteboarding.com
- *Kiteboarding Magazine*
- World Kitesurfing Organization
  www.kite-surf.net

LONG DISTANCE SWIMMING
- Channel Swimming Association
  Sunnybank
  Alkham Valley Rd.,
  Folkestone, Kent CT18 7EH, UK
  Tel: (0044) 303 892229
  Fax: (0044) 303 891033

SCUBA DIVING
- SSI
  2619 Canton Court,
  Ft. Collons, CO 80525-4498
  Tel: (001) 970 482 0883
  Fax: (001) 970 482 6157
- N. O. B. (Netherlands)
  Nassaustraat 12, 3583 XG Utrecht,
  Holland

WATER. NINETY PER CENT of our bodies are made of it. Two-thirds of the planet is covered by it. It is the most inhospitable of the the earth's elements for human survival, yet without it, life would cease. If indeed all life began in the water, as modern theories of evolution suggest, perhaps this explains why we are so attracted to it, and why being in or near it fosters a sense of synergy. It welcomes us through some ethereal sense of belonging, and we respond by seeking to find any way we can to have fun in and on it. For as long as there has been human life, there have been opportunities for sport in the water.

For centuries stories have been told about the terrible demise of sailors eaten by mammoth sea creatures. A legacy of artwork depicting scenes of horror, with monsters eating entire ships full of people, speaks volumes about how far from fearful superstition we have come. Many of the mysteries surrounding the depths of the oceans and lakes covering the planet have long been solved.

Sailboats are now built to be raced on courses that circumnavigate the globe. Consider that it was only 500 years ago that Columbus successfully crossed the Atlantic and found the New World, a trip that is now made daily in only hours by jet.

A DANGEROUS ELEMENT

Yet the oceans still have many dangers, both seen and unseen. Rocks or reefs clearly visible at a low tide might lie just beneath the water's surface at high tide. Being aware of them by seeing and understanding the clues they leave on the water's surface when they are submerged is a valuable skill, whether surfing or sailing. Being able to avoid them, especially at speed, can mean the difference between life and death.

Beneath the surface, the risks are far greater, ranging from being attacked by aggressive or hungry sea dwellers to falling prey to any one of several things that go wrong when using a

breathing apparatus. Human beings were not meant to survive under water, and by exploring its depths we leave ourselves exposed and vulnerable.

Rivers hold many of the same hidden dangers, yet they occur with such frequency that avoiding them is actually the sport. It is the rocks and boulders that give whitewater its name, not just the speed at which the water travels, and athletes wishing to test their abilities must be able to react quickly and decisively if they are to survive life-threatening situations.

When struck at speed, water takes on properties that are closer to cement than any liquid. The water's surface texture is ever-changing, creating opportunities for jumping, often at inappropriate times. Some sources for jumping are also sources of propulsion; such is the case with waves for boardsailors and surfers, who view surf very differently.

A VARIED CHALLENGE

How each athlete views water is as different as the sports they pursue. Large swells and waves make for great surfing, but without breeze, poor boardsailing. A strong breeze makes for great boardsailing, but strong winds can ruin an incredible surf day by changing the waves from clean and smooth to messy and chopped up.

What makes these water sports extreme is that each was created by redefining the limits of what was possible in terms of human and technological performance on and under the water. Anyone wishing to know how long a swimmer can stay submerged or how far a swimmer can travel under their own power can look to these sports for answers. That is because someone made it their task and their passion to find out for themselves what they were capable of doing in or on water.

■ ANU SCUBA Club (Australia)
 Tel: (0061) 06 249 3490
■ Ontario Underwater Explorers (Canada)
 contact Anthony Deboer
 e-mail: (home) abd@herboid.reptiles.org
 (work) abd@geac.com
 Tel: (001) 905 508 4718
■ NYC Sea Gypsies (New York, U.S.)
 e-mail: HarryW5594@aol.com
 Tel: (001) 212 753 6603
■ Santa Clarita Dive Club
 25335 Via Ramon,
 Valencia, CA 91355
 e-mail: xdcuste@dwp.la.ca.us
■ Dive Club 854 (Singapore)
 Blk 510,
 West Coast Drive, #09-319
 Singapore, 0512
 e-mail jgfsegny@technet.sg
 (include phrase "To Tan Tsu Soo")
■ SCUBA Times (magazine)
 14110 Peridido Key Dr., ste #16
 Pensacola, FL 32507
 Tel: (001) 904 492 7605
 Fax: (001) 904 492 7607
■ *SCUBA Diving* (magazine)
 http://www.scubadiving.com
 6600 Abercorn St., Suite 208,
 Savannah, GA 31405
 Tel: (001) 912 351 08550
 Fax: (001) 912 351 07550

SPEED SAILING
■ U.S. Sailing Association
 PO Box 1260,
 Portsmouth, RI 02871
 Fax: (001) 401 683 0840
 75530.502@compuserve.com
■ Yacht Racing Union International
 60 Knightsbridge,
 London SW1X 7JX, UK
 Tel: (0044) 711235 9861

SURFING
■ International Surfing Association
 5580 La Jolla Blvd, Suite 145,
 La Jolla CA 92037
 Tel: (001) 619 691 6893
 Fax: (001) 619 691 0594
■ U.S. Surfing Federation
 Kiernon and Angiulo
 350 Jericho Turnpike,
 Jericho, NY 11753
 Tel: (001) 516 935 0400
 Fax: (001) 516 942 4705
■ European Surfing Federation
 45 Long Cram,
 Haddington, Lothian EH41 4NS
 Scotland
 Tel: (0044) 62 0823973
 Fax: (0044) 62 0823973
■ *Surfing Magazine*
 33046 Calle Aviador,
 San Juan Capistrano, CA 92675
 Tel: (001) 714 496 5922
 Fax: (001) 714 496 7849
 Subscription dept. *Surfing Magazine*
 PO Box 54970
 Boulder, CO 80322-4970
 Tel: (001) 800 879 0484

WAKEBOARDING
■ *Wakeboarding* (magazine)
 330 W Canton, Winter Park, FL 32789
 Tel: (001) 407 628 4802
 Fax: (001) 407 628 7061
 http://www.rio.com/ wakezone/
■ *Interactive Guide to Wakeboarding*
 (CD-ROM)
 Tel: (001) 800 599 8856

WHITEWATER RAFTING
■ Nepal Association of Rafting Agents
 PO Box 3586,
 Kamaladi,
 Kathmandu, Nepal
 Tel: (00977) 220714
 Fax: (00977) 226021
■ Wyoming River Raiders (retailers)
 601 Wyoming River Blvd.
 Casper, WY 82609
 catalog: (001) 800 247 6068
■ The American Whitewater Affiliation
 PO Box 636,
 16 Bull Run Rd.
 Margaretville, NY 12455
 e-mail: 74663.2104@compuserve.com
 Tel: (001) 914 586 2355
 Fax: (001) 914 586 3050

Air Chair

The hydrofoil, a wing that creates lift in water, is not new, and hydrofoils are commonly used on powerboats today. They are even used on sailboats to minimize resistance and set speed records, which is itself an extreme endeavor. However, it wasn't until 1989 that a hydrofoil attached to a chair became commercially available for athletes seeking a new tow-behind water challenge.

THE AIR CHAIR, as it has become known, was designed by a couple of friends on the Colorado River, one of whom was the co-creator of the kneeboard (a waterski that the rider kneels on) and a hot dog waterski pioneer, Mike Murphy. Murphy's friend Bob Wooley became fascinated with the concept of riding a performance hydrofoil, and after several months of experimentation attached the foil to a "sit ski," a seated version of a waterski.

The seated foil rig was promising, and Wooley continued refining the design with Murphy. In 1989 they started the Air Chair company, and since then have sold thousands of Air Chairs. The device has proved popular for its radical spinning and flipping moves as well as the ease with which they can be learned. One of the sports pioneers and trick innovators is Tony Klarich, who has created a number of moves that are now considered standard.

The Air Chair is basically a sit ski (top), with the addition of a simple hydrofoil (left). This has created an incredibly mobile and enjoyable device which, despite appearances (below) is relatively easy to ride.

Everyone's sport

The Air Chair is relatively easy to ride since once the foil is working the rig creates minimal drag. Jet-propelled personal watercraft and small boats with as little as 25 hp can tow the Air Chair. These advantages enable a broader spectrum of water sports enthusiasts to enjoy the device.

It is physically far easier to ride an Air Chair than it is to ski, kneeboard, or wakeboard. What makes the Air Chair extreme is that it uses technology to push the limits of performance. Reportedly the Air Chair is capable of attaining so much air in a jump that the only limitation on one's ability to achieve maximum air is mental. The foil breaks the shock of the landings, so impact is always pretty cushy and comfortable.

As a testament to how easy the device is to ride, Murphy's 77-year-old mother, Mary, rides an Air Chair. Whether or not she launches 20-foot (6m) jumps like Mike is another question. So while the Air Chair may not be the most physically challenging extreme sport, it is technologically cool enough to grab the attention of most extreme athletes.

Barefoot Water Skiing

Sports are about competition, but also about contact. Sports which involve the thrill of speed invariably require specialized equipment to undertake them, but for the sportsman, the nearer to the elements you can get, the greater the sense of accomplishment. So for water skiers, what could make more sense than dispensing with the skis?

BAREFOOT WATER SKIING began in Winter Haven, Florida in 1947. Water skiing pioneer Chuck Sligh theorized that water skiing without skis might be possible if the ski boat went fast enough. A 17-year-old boy named AG Hancock proved him right, becoming the first water skier to drop a ski and continue barefoot successfully. Hancock left on a family vacation before he could show the trick to Cypress Garden's Dick Pope Sr.. A few days later, Pope's son Dick Jr. successfully dropped a ski and got all the glory— photographs, newspaper stories, newsreels, the works. Barefoot skiers soon adapted many of the freestyle moves of traditional waterskiers. Spins, backward maneuvers, body drags, and other tricks made barefooting an exciting new discipline. Due to the speeds required to barefoot, the tricks are especially difficult, and dangerous, since the water becomes very hard in a high-speed impact.

Barefoot water skiing quickly became a cult sport, especially in Australia. Barefoot clubs and competitions took place throughout the Sixties without too many people outside of the sport taking notice. Sometime around 1967 the Australians began experimenting with barefoot jumping. No one knows who the first barefoot jumper was, but he set in motion a chain of events that eventually brought his sport some long-overdue attention.

In 1973, the Australians introduced the Americans to barefoot jumping at the International Championships, held at Cypress Gardens. It wasn't until 1978 that jumping was included as an event at the first U.S. Barefoot Nationals. That same year Greg Rees of Australia set the first official world record at 44 feet (13.41m).

Bum jumpers

The techniques used at this time were foot-to-foot, where the jumper used his feet for both the take-off and the landing, and something called bum jumping. Bum jumpers went up and off the ramp on their buttocks and then tried to land on their feet, a technique that resulted in longer jumps, but was uncontrollable.

Even this spectacle wasn't enough to garner a lot of mainstream attention. That all changed in 1989 when U.S. jumper Mike Seipel accidentally invented the inverted style of jumping while training in Florida.

The first time it happened Seipel says the thought that occurred to him was "I'm going to kill myself," so he let go of the handle and splashed in. Then he realized that he had flown farther, so he tried it again, sticking the landing on his third try.

In the inverted style, the jumper pushes forward at the top of the ramp and lets the handle out. This puts the jumper horizontal to the water, flying most of the distance of the jump in that position, then swinging his body back down for a landing, hopefully on his feet and buttocks. The first time Seipel tried it in competition he broke the world record, flying 72.5 feet (22.10m).

The sport immediately exploded. Jumpers who were initially skeptical of the new technique quickly learned it, and average jumps went from 40–50 feet up to 60–70 feet. The current record of 90.88 feet (27.70m) is held by Australian Justin Sears, and the 100 foot mark is expected to fall soon.

Opposite: Mike Seipel demonstrates his 'accidental' inverted style of jumping. Right:Marc Alexander of France shows what effect it had on him.

Boardsailing

Since it was first introduced to readers in a 1965 edition of *Popular Science* magazine, boardsailing has developed into one of the most visible and incredible of extreme sports. There is hardly a person alive who hasn't seen an athlete hurtling across the water or jumping into the sky on a wind-powered board.

THE SAILBOARD was invented by California surfer and businessman Hoyle Schweitzer and aeronautical engineer Jim Drake. Schweitzer reportedly conceived of the idea of putting a sail on a surfboard while Drake created the articulating sail rig that made the concept feasible. The two promptly applied for, and were granted, patents on their design and began the company that would be known worldwide as Windsurfer. For quite a while, the sport was known as "windsurfing," but because of trademark litigation, the growing industry renamed their sport "boardsailing." Either name is acceptable.

The original Windsurfer was a 12-foot (3.65m) long, heavy board made from pressure-molded ABS plastic. The boards were rough and their sail rigs were unrefined, using wooden booms (what the sailor holds onto) and inefficient sails. However, the sensation for early sailors was incredibly exciting and unlike what any other sailing vessel, including fast and exciting catamarans, could offer. Soon there were Windsurfers everywhere, and races began to be organized by enthusiasts. New equipment developed, including "harnesses" that allowed boardsailors to "hook in and hold on" for longer sessions with less fatigue.

Jean-Luc Vasse of France rides the big waves of Hookipa in Hawaii, widely regarded as the best wavesailing water in the world.

The exuberance of boardsailing is gaining the sport more and more popularity in all parts of the world.

Footstraps have ensured that being "slammed" is less likely for boardsailors.

The early harnesses had hooks on the chest that grabbed lines tied to the booms of the sail rig. Back fatigue and injuries resulted in a new "seat" harness designed to give better leverage and control over the rig, and decrease stresses placed on the sailor's back. But a problem the harness created was that a sailor hit by a large gust of wind, or off balance, could be catapulted forward and slammed into the water, or worse, into the board itself. Harnesses are now standard equipment for any boardsailor, however the opportunity to get slammed has not gone away.

Strapped for effect

The first groundbreaking modifications to Windsurfers were made by Hawaiian surfers. They started adding to their boards with footstraps and sails, and modern wavesailing was born. Early pioneers like Robby Naish are still leading athletes today. Windsurfer responded by creating their Rocket series of mass-production boards with footstraps and modified hulls. These boards were still heavy compared to the light fiberglass custom surfboard designs, but to the tens of thousands of people already boardsailing they delivered the thrill of sailing "strapped."

Robby Seeger charges down a massive face in the huge sea around Hawaii.

Footstraps delivered a new dimension of control to boardsailing, allowing sailors to stay on their boards in winds that would have previously thrown them—being "slammed" became far less frequent. Being able to gain a more secure footing also let strong sailors break into new speed territory. Soon enough high-wind sailing made moderate winds look boring to extreme athletes, and the bigger heavy boards became the dinosaurs of boardsailing.

Riding a sinker

Custom and mass-produced performance boards became the "must have" equipment for expert boardsailors. As with many speed sports, lighter means faster, and stiffer means better control. Sailboarders seeking to sail in extreme conditions of high wind, or high wind and surf, found that once their boards were moving, they no longer required big boards. In fact, big hulls became unstable in high winds since the wind would constantly seek to rip the board away from the water and sailor. Smaller boards were easily made lighter, and those that could get started on them could do circles around other sailors. The smaller the boards became, the less buoyancy

they offered, to the point at which they no longer supported the sailor's weight unless they were moving and could ride on top of the water.

Riders wishing to sail these "sinkers" had to learn to do a "water start." In a water start, because the board cannot float with the sailor on it, the sailor lies in the water waiting for the sail to pick them up onto the board. As the sailor gets lifted up, the board begins moving, increasing its ability to support his weight. As the board accelerates, it planes (rides on top) on the water's surface, and is able to travel with little resistance. The sailor must keep the sail

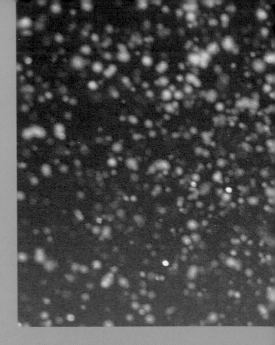

Forward loops, though still spectacular, are now standard fare for the world's top boardsailors.

properly trimmed (adjusted) to maximize the amount of force the available wind can give to move the board. Therefore, the better the sailor is at trimming the sail, the faster the board will travel.

Top experts can get their boards to travel at their maximum velocity for the wind and water conditions. The rest is a matter of strength and handling ability. An expert can steer the board with foot movement and weight transfer, using the board's rails (edges) to carve turns.

Board designs vary as to their maneuverability. Boards with straighter shapes and sharp (close to 90-degree angle) rails release the water from the bottom of the board better

136

Robby Naish has been a top boardsailor for many years.

France's Jenne de Rosnay showing the complete control necessary for today's top performers.

and attain higher speeds, but are more difficult to turn, as they have a tendency to skip out of a hard turn. Boards with rounder shapes and loose (rounded) rails are highly maneuverable but don't go as fast.

Maintaining control

Boards also vary in rocker (the amount the bottom curves from the tip to tail of the board). Rocker placement varies from board to board, and on each board. Boards with more rocker in the tail will be slower but more maneuverable, while boards with less tail rocker will plane quicker and go faster. Each board designer places rocker in different places determined by the performance desired, and each boardsailor prefers a different feel and shape.

Early "short" board designs looked more like surfboards than today's top shapes. Board buoyancy is measured by volume, so less volume means less floatation. Designers shift the volume around in their boards, placing more or less in the tip or tail dramatically effects performance. Short boards started out with massive amounts of volume in the tail. One early design by top boardsailor Ken Winner actually had a hump though the middle of the rear deck of the board, and a pointy front. Designers gradually reduced the volume in the back of the boards, moving it forward under the mast base.

The volume-forward shapes were the predominant style of short boards until the early Nineties, when designers discovered they could reduce the length and increase

board performance by centering the volume under the sailor, much like Winner's early design, but without the hump. The "no nose" designs have greatly reduced volume in the front, with much of the rail shape occurring farther back in the board. Essentially what they've done is to use a very short board and lengthen the tip to create a moderately short board. Either way, these boards are a vast improvement over designs only a few years old.

Getting up, of course, requires getting down, and top experts are in control during flight, using their sail as a wing to float down to the water. What boardsailors can do in the air has changed dramatically over the years as equipment has changed and sailors have redefined the limits of performance.

Nik Baker windsurfing in Hawaii, USA.

France's Robert Teritehau has helped redefine the limits of boardsailing performance.

360 degree spins are also possible and visually stunning.

there. When considering buying used gear keep in mind that the sail and rig are the "engine," and therefore the most important items. Even an old ugly board can out-perform a new one if the sails are better or equal. Look for signs of excessive wear on the cloth like abrasions, cuts, repairs, and stretched or threadbare seams. Any combination of these can point to a terrible sail. The only-true way to tell if a sail is good is to rig it and look at the shape. Those who can't tell a good shape from a bad one should ask an experienced friend to help. The shape should look curved like an airplane wing.

The best sites

Sailing sites vary in their appeal. Some sites, like Hookipa on Maui, are world-renowned for their huge waves and high winds. Hookipa is widely regarded as the best wavesailing in the world, since it offers high winds running at 90 degrees to the large Hawaiian surf, allowing expert sailors to sail full speed into the huge faces and shoot as high as 30 feet (9m) in the air. Another great sailing site is the Columbia River Gorge in Oregon, where the wind roars at up to 60 mph (96kph) up the river against a current heading the other way. The strong current and wind work together to create huge rolling waves, which attract thousands of sailors in the late summer each year. Other heavily visited sites include the Canary Islands, Southern France, Southern Spain, and the Caribbean.

Tricks like "forward loops" (front flip) are now standard fare for top experts. In a forward loop, the sailor goes as fast as possible into a wave and, while airborne, pulls hard on the sail at the same time as leaping forward. This highly technical trick is amazing to watch—360-degree spins are also possible and exciting.

Rigged to wing it

One of the best technological advances in boardsailing was the introduction of the R.A.F. (Rotating Aerodynamic Foil) and Camber-Inducing batten systems. The R.A.F. system was the first to be introduced, and it allowed sails to take on more rigid, wing-like shapes when rigged. R.A.F. design made sails far easier to handle in high and gusty wind conditions because they created smoother shapes with less drag. Drag pulls on a sail, sometimes violently, and decreases top end velocity. Camber Inducers were introduced when sailmakers added enough length to the sail's battens (fiberglass or composite sticks that add stability to the sail's shape) to connect them to the mast that supports the sail. Camber Inducers allowed sailmakers to design rigid shapes that are incredibly efficient and easy to handle. The softer R.A.F. designs are best used in the waves, while Camber sails are best used for speed, as they are more fragile and easily damaged in surf.

Owning the equipment is not cheap if bought new, however, good used stuff is out

One of the great things about boardsailing is that all you need is water, wind, and a board. The fun is just part of the deal. Just about anyone who can swim can boardsail. Anyone brave enough to seek a little instruction will find it is remarkably easy to do if you know a few basics of how the set-up works. Once a new sailor has learned how to get up and ride a sailboard, the trip from big board to short board sailing isn't long. All that's needed is some time and patience, and a little perseverance.

Freediving

Swimming into the deepest reaches of the ocean is a feat that many divers have experienced to a degree. Some may go below 200 feet (60m), others deeper. All would be lost without the air they bring with them. There is a special breed of diver who can go deeper than most, without air tanks. These freedivers have pushed the limits of unassisted breathing dives to below 400 feet.

TO FREEDIVE TO DEPTHS of even 50 feet (15m) is an unsettling prospect for all but the strongest swimmers. To dive much deeper requires holding a breath for minutes. In fact, the world's best freedivers hold their breath for periods that rival many marine mammals.

There are three categories of freediving for depth. First there is "fixed weight" or "fixed volume" diving. Divers in this discipline swim down as deep as they can under their own power, and resurface the same way. This means using up valuable air in the descent, limiting the speed at which they can get deep, and the depths attainable. The current record is over 240 feet (73m), and was set by Frenchman Eric Charrier in 1995. Fixed weight divers use high-technology composite swim fins to aid them in going down and coming up.

Second is "variable weight" freediving, in which ballast is used to aid divers descend; up to one-third of body weight is considered legal. Variable weight divers can get down faster and with less effort than fixed weight divers, yet they must still swim back to the surface under their own power. Again the use of special fins is a requirement.

Third is called "absolute" diving, which allows unlimited ballast in the descent, with rates reaching between 12–15 feet per second (3.65–4.6m). To return to the surface, the diver grabs a lifting aid, such as an inflatable bag. Cuban diver Francisco "Pepin" Ferreras-Rodriguez holds the current record at 417 feet (127m), an amazing depth. Pepin boasts an extraordinary lung capacity, and has been freediving since age seven.

Advanced breathing

How divers like Pepin reach these depths is by learning to control their body's ability to sustain them between breaths. But regardless of how it is done, prolonged periods between breaths can result in latent hypoxia, or "shallow water blackout." Ironically, shallow water blackout occurs usually just below the surface and the diver can drown if unassisted. Many use advanced breathing methods, like the Tai'Chi yoga breathing technique. These methods aid the divers in controlling and even reducing the rate of their metabolism, thus decreasing the need for oxygen. Another—though less zen-related method—is to hyperventilate. This involves prolonged deep breathing before the dive, which increases the ratio of oxygen in the lungs and effectively "tricks" the body into lowering its need to breathe so frequently. This is not as effective as meditation.

Freedivers must economize their movement in order to maximize their time underwater. Each move requires oxygen, and there is clearly a limited supply. Good divers don't rush the process and, as a result, can remain underwater for longer periods.

Freediving embodies the extreme athlete's quest for inner control and improved performance in sports. Without question, a failed attempt can end in death and, as with so many other extreme sports, the athlete must be fully prepared both mentally and physically if they are to succeed.

Freediving is the province of the few.
It embodies the athlete's quest for
inner control and improved performance
under the most difficult circumstances.
Superb swimming skills, mental and
physical preparation are essential for
successful and safe freediving.

Jet Skiing

Motorcycles have always attracted people with a yearning for speed and an appetite for adrenaline. For years, the closest thing anyone could get to that sensation on the water was in a small boat with a big motor. These were fast, but could hardly be called maneuverable. Then in 1965 a Californian banker with a passion for motorcycles conceived of an aquatic version which would become known worldwide as the Jet Ski.

CLAYTON JACOBSON enjoyed building racing motorcycles in his spare time. He loved going fast on motorcycles—but crashing on hard pavement was not what he considered to be their appeal. The concept of the Jet Ski was born from Jacobson's theory that a motorcycle for the water would be just as fun to ride as the ones he enjoyed building, but without the pain of a hard landing if you fell off. Mr. Jacobson would be correct.

Jacobson built a few prototypes from his designs, and after being issued a patent in 1969, licensed his design to Ski-Doo manufacturer Bombardier. Bombardier ran into several problems and halted development a year later. Their license to use the design expired in 1971, and within months Jacobson signed a deal with Kawasaki to use his design. In 1973 Kawasaki introduced the Jet Ski, the first stand-up personal watercraft. Clayton Jacobson's concept soon became one of the most successful boat designs in history.

What made the Jet Ski possible was that Jacobson utilized a jet water-pump system rather then the Sixties state-of-the-art inboard or outboard motor propulsion systems. These motors utilize an external propeller to provide thrust. The Jet Ski design uses an internal water-jet motor for thrust. The motor draws water into itself and shoots a stream out again to generate thrust, without exposing potentially hazardous blades that can injure a rider. Current engines deliver in excess of 85

Jet skiing events are broken down into three classes. The first (above) is the Runabout, designed for craft that seat more than one person. The second (below) is the Sport Division with lighter, higher performance craft, and the third (right) is the Ski Division designed for one stand-up rider.

horsepower and can push the Jet Ski to speeds exceeding 50 mph (80kph).

The correct term for the jet-driven craft currently available is "personal watercraft." The term Jet Ski is a registered trademark of the Kawasaki Corporation. Kawasaki had exclusive domain over the jet-driven personal watercraft until 1987, when several would-be rivals entered the market with sit-down versions. Because the sit-down design is far less physically demanding than the stand-up Jet Ski, they have far broader consumer appeal, and now make up over 95 per cent of the personal watercraft market.

Both stand-up and sit-down designs offer a sense of freedom and performance that is unrivaled by other small motorized boats. They allow riders to use their bodies to enhance the watercraft's performance. Much like the motorcycles they were intended to replicate, personal watercraft give riders a wind-and-water-in-the-face sensation that is addictive to say the least.

Racing and freestyle

Competitive events are held internationally, and include closed-course racing and freestyle riding. The freestyle events are meant to showcase each rider's skills by requiring them to execute a series of difficult and creative maneuvers within a predetermined time period, generally two minutes. Each rider is scored by a panel of seven judges, issuing points from 1–10. The rider with the highest score wins. Riders execute a range of tricks, including submerging their watercraft and shooting it up out of the water, as well as jumps and spins requiring strength and agility.

The closed-course races require groups of riders to race each other around a set of buoys, with the winner determined at the finish line. The closed courses include a series of right- and left-hand turns, requiring riders to be strong all-around drivers. These races take place as a series of elimination heats. The top finishers advance to the next race until a group reaches the final heat. The finishing positions in the final heat determine the overall winners.

Events are broken down into three classes. First is the Runabout Division, consisting of sit-down personal watercraft designed to seat one or more. Second is the Sport Division, which uses lighter, higher-performance versions of sit-down watercraft. Third is the Ski Division, which comprises stand-up designs for one rider.

Safety first

In many ways personal watercraft have redefined water activities and their costs. These vehicles average around $8,550 (£5,700), bringing a new affordability to performance watercraft. This is especially inexpensive when you consider that many outboard motors of similar horsepower cost around the same price without the boat attached.

Because they were designed to be fallen from, each personal watercraft has at least one of two safety devices built in. First is an automatic steering mechanism to direct the watercraft in circles after a rider has fallen off. Second is a cord that is attached to the driver and the ignition system. If the rider falls off, the engine turns off and the watercraft awaits the swimming driver.

Even these safety devices cannot replace commonsense. All personal watercraft riders should wear floatation devices, and a helmet is a good idea too, when extreme riding. Many drivers like to spin their boats around and travel at high speed close to other riders, and often in opposing

One of the latest developments of the sport is indoor "Super Jet Ski" competitions like this one in Paris, France. Spectators are never too far from the spectacular action.

directions. Top experts may be capable of doing this with reasonable control, but novices should consider staying away from other watercraft, especially other novices, The craft are heavy, travel at deceptively high speeds, and collisions can have terrible consequences.

Jet-drive watercraft are used for a range of sports today, including waterskiing, wake-boarding, and—most dramatically—tow-in surfing, a sport that started in the massive waves off Maui, Hawaii, where personal watercraft drivers can quickly tow surfers on narrow high-performance surfboards out to big waves that would be unsurfable if the

surfers weren't moving before the wave caught them.

The popularity of personal watercraft is underscored by the frequency with which they are visible at beaches and on waterways around the world. There is not a beach resort anywhere that doesn't have at least one available for rent. The reason seems obvious, personal watercraft allow boaters and non-boaters the opportunity to get out on the water and experience a sense of freedom that was previously only reserved for motorcyclists.

Closed-course races around buoys requires the successful navigation of tight right- and left-hand turns.

Kiteboarding

For years, pioneering sailors have played with the concept of winglike sails in the never ending pursuit of greater performance. Early designs utilized hang-glider-like sails in an effort to reharness the sideways forces a sail's winglike shape generates. This sideways force known as lift, pushes sailcraft sideways as well as propelling them forward. The basic theory is to generate upward lift and forward thrust which would allow for lighter, faster, and more efficient hull designs.

Ben Hanbury gets wet kite surfing at Watergate Bay in Cornwall.

THESE EFFORTS lead to the use of ram air type parachutes designed for skydivers seeking maneuverability, speed, and lift. The impressive lift generated by these chutes coupled with their ability to be steered and stability at speed made them ideal for designs capable of attaining high speeds. On the list of obvious candidates were windsurfers and the sport of kiteboarding was born.

Kiteboarding required further development of the ram air design, including the ability to deploy the wing from a standing start in the water. The high lift generated by the kites allowed sailors to get pulled up out of the water. Kite and board designs got better and smaller, and soon innovators were using wakeboards and new designs with little to no bouyancy.

Soon, top boardsailors like Robby Naish, five-times World Boardsailing Champion and 2000 World Kiteboarding Champion, joined in the effort to push kiteboard design further. Today, kiteboarders continue to redefine the limits of performance in this new sport.

Spectacular jumps make the biggest airs achieved by boardsailors look small in comparison.

Known as "Big Steps", kiteboarding jumps are augmented by the tremendous lift the kites generate. Kiteboarders can steer their kites forward and use the lift to pull them ahead at great speeds. As they hit a big wave, or even in smaller "choppy" waves, boarders can steer their kites up into "neutral" position where only upward lift is generated. The result is that kiteboarders then have massive vertical jumping capabilities and long, long, long hang time.

Open Water Swimming

Swimming long distances for sport is a challenge that only the most fit and determined extreme athletes pursue. Its roots can be traced back to 1875 when Captain Matthew Webb became the first swimmer to cross the English Channel. Since then, crossing the channel has been one of the more defining feats of long distance, or open water, swimming. Open water is the appropriate term, since races and crossings are never held in a pool, that would be too easy and lacking danger.

OPEN WATER SWIMMING races are held globally, and were included in many of the early Olympic Games. Course lengths are usually 5, 10, 15, or 25 kilometers (3–15.5 miles) and require several hours to complete. The courses are set between two points on any large body of water. Some races require athletes to do several laps to complete a given distance, while others may consist of one very long lap.

Open water swimming may seem like an individual achievement, however open water swimmers always work with a coach, who travels nearby in a boat. The coach's job is to monitor the swimmer's performance, give feedback, and insure the swimmer doesn't get into danger while competing. The coach's boat also doubles as a rescue craft.

Although apparently a individual's sport, long distance swimmers cannot do without the support of a coach, who will offer encouragement, food and even the occasional drink.

Swimmers can come across several natural hazards during the course of an event, ranging from life-threatening sea creatures to debris and rough water. The coach endeavors to guide the swimmer around any hazards. A common hazard is jellyfish. The threat of being stung is ever present, and given that most stings occur directly on the face and neck, a most unpleasant event. Another is sharks.

When a shark is sighted, swimmers naturally react by swimming faster out of added adrenaline. Attacks, however, are not common, and it is the coach's duty to assess any shark presence for signs of aggressive behavior.

Swimmers are not allowed to wear any kind of wetsuit, so hypothermia (becoming super-cold) is a key concern during any event. Again, it is the duty of the coach to determine if the swimmer is becoming hypothermic, and if so to encourage them to work harder to boost their body temperature. If the swimmer is unable to combat hypothermia, it is the coach's job to get them out of the water and retire from the race, a task that is not always as easy as it sounds.

Physical demands

Open water swimmers must be in tremendous physical condition in order to deal with the demands these events put upon them. Athletes must train constantly, with little opportunity for diversity. The stamina and pain thresholds for each athlete must be at maximum for them to be competitive. Swimmers must maintain effort through rough and cold water, persevere in difficult currents, tidal surges, and wind-driven waves. Any one of these can cause the contestant to lose way, even lose some of the distance they've worked so hard to cover.

Open water swimming is an extreme endurance event in which only the most determined succeed.

Powerboat Racing

Creating vehicles capable of traveling at fantastic speeds has been one of the common goals of extreme sports for as long as the technology to do so has existed. Not very long ago, motorized boats capable of 30–40 mph (48–64kph) were considered fast. Now the technology of boat construction and the horsepower available to the engines has given us power boats able to exceed 140 mph (225kph).

THE DRIVING FORCE in the quest for powerboat speed has been racing. Since the first powerboat sped across the English Channel in 1903, the quest for speed has pushed powerboat technology forward tremendously. That sprint from Calais, France to Dover, England took place on a 39-foot (12m) hull powered by a 75 horse power Daimler engine. Pleasure boaters can use that kind of power plant on one of many small, light fiberglass boats commercially available without even blinking. Open-class racing boats today boast horse power ratings of over 1000.

Powerboats use two different types of engine. The first and original power plant is the "inboard" engine. Inboards are placed in the middle of the hull and turn a propeller via a driveshaft that passes through the hull toward the stern of the boat. Still widely used in racing, inboards offer a low center of gravity which improves the boat's stability.

Hulled for speed

Second is the "outboard." Outboards are essentially lightweight units clamped to the transom (the vertical plane at the stern). Outboards are commonly used to power smaller racing hulls and pleasure boats, and because they are compact and outside the hull, their use creates more room for gear and occupants. The drawback is the height of the weight placement of the motor, and the placement of the weight so far back in the hull. This makes outboard-powered hulls less

(Above) Outboard powerboat racing is popular as it is at the cheaper end of the powerboat spectrum. Unlike the modern racing "cats" (below) which have to exist in the corporate world of the sponsor.

stable than inboard-powered, especially when the motors are proportionately large compared to the boat.

Racing boats utilize three distinct hull designs. First is the "Deep V" originated by U.S. designer Dick Bertram. The hull has a V-shape running through the hull's center from the bow (front) to the stern (rear). The angle of the V is sharp at the bow and gradually tapers to a flatter angle at the stern. A series of "steps" runs the length of the hull, and provides lift and stability. Bertram's Deep V

changed the powerboat world virtually overnight after winning the 1960 Miami Nassau Race in a record eight hours. The design, with its sharp angles forward and stepped hull, allowed his boat to travel faster in rougher conditions than the flatter, unstepped hulls of the period. Today, almost every modern V-hull utilizes Bertram's design.

Cats and foils

Second is a catamaran design consisting of two very sharp V-hulls mounted side by side. Modern

racing "cats" are more efficient and therefore require less horsepower than the single V-hull design. Where races allow both V- and cat-hulls to compete, more powerful engines are usually allowed in the V-hull designs to offset the cats' advantage in efficiency.

Third is the hydrofoil design, which uses a wide, flat hull and two shallow asymmetrical cat-style hulls mounted forward and outside of the flat central hull. Used only in flat-water areas, these boats use tremendous horsepower to accelerate out of the turns in what are

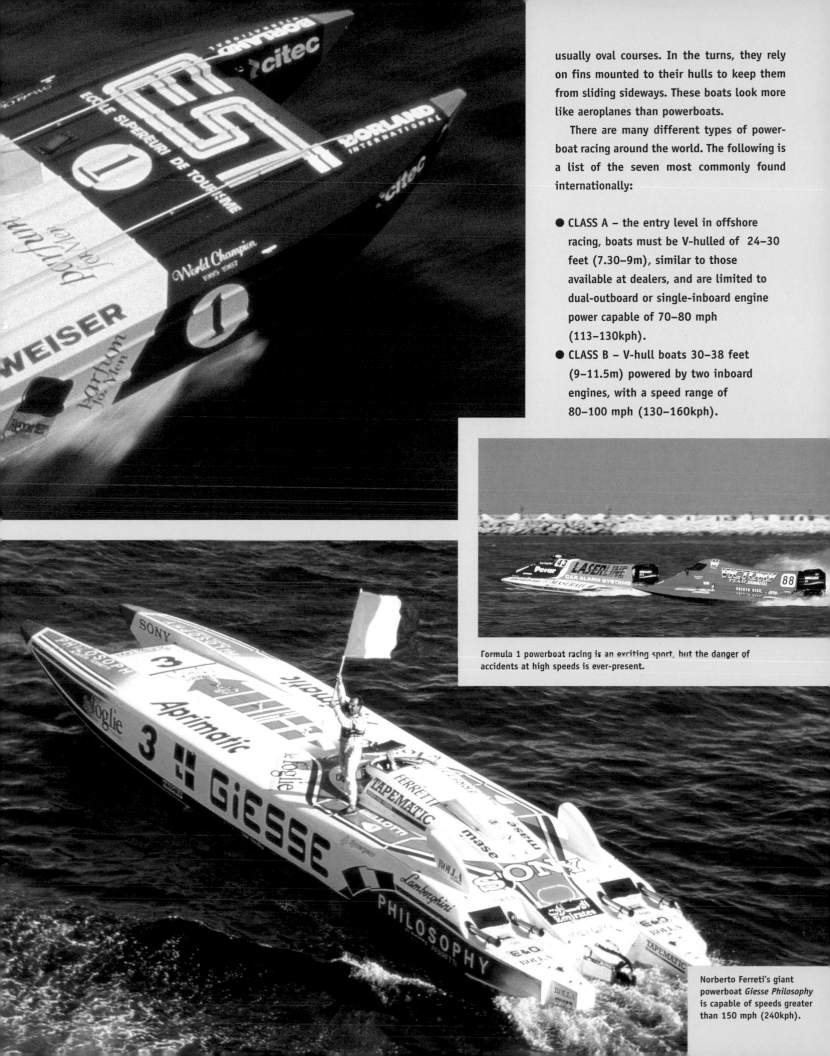

usually oval courses. In the turns, they rely on fins mounted to their hulls to keep them from sliding sideways. These boats look more like aeroplanes than powerboats.

There are many different types of power-boat racing around the world. The following is a list of the seven most commonly found internationally:

● CLASS A – the entry level in offshore racing, boats must be V-hulled of 24–30 feet (7.30–9m), similar to those available at dealers, and are limited to dual-outboard or single-inboard engine power capable of 70–80 mph (113–130kph).
● CLASS B – V-hull boats 30–38 feet (9–11.5m) powered by two inboard engines, with a speed range of 80–100 mph (130–160kph).

Formula 1 powerboat racing is an exciting sport, but the danger of accidents at high speeds is ever-present.

Norberto Ferreti's giant powerboat *Giesse Philosophy* is capable of speeds greater than 150 mph (240kph).

The hydrofoil design gives tremendous extra power for accelerating out of turns, the hull fins also keep them from sliding sideways.

- CLASS C – catamarans of 28–30 feet (8.5–9m) powered by two outboard engines capable of between 100–110 mph (160–177kph)—consistently one of the most evenly matched classes.
- CLASS P – "pro stock" racers, all cat designs of 30–38 feet (9–11.5m), with three outboard engines and top speeds averaging 100–115 mph.
- CLASS M – "Modified" class hulls can be either cat or V design. V hulls are allowed to carry more

horsepower due to the efficiency advantage cat hulls have.
- OPEN CLASS – hulls generally in excess of 35 feet (11m), with engines of 1,000 horsepower and greater, capable of around 135 mph (217kph)—the premier class of offshore racing.
- UNLIMITED CLASS – unlimited hydrofoils—the fastest of powerboat racers, but their designs confine them to the calm waters of lakes and protected shore regions—are powered by inboards, outboards, and even jet engines capable of speeds exceeding 150 mph (240kph).

Powerboats are prone to violent crashes, mostly due to the unlevel surface of water. If hit at high speed, water behaves more like cement that you would imagine.

Offshore racing boats have a crew of two or three in order to effectively manage their hulls at speed. The driver must concentrate solely on steering and keeping the boat under control, while an additional crew member controls the throttle and navigates. A third may be onboard as navigator for the larger Open Class boats.

Powerboats are prone to violent crashes, largely thanks to inconsistent water surfaces. Even small waves hitting the hull in an odd or unexpected way are capable of sending boats flying out of the water where they become like uncontrollable aircraft. Sometimes landings can be smooth, but backward flips and hard impacts are more likely. And because of the excessive speeds, the results can be deadly—at 100+ mph, water behaves like cement.

Engine fires, fuel fires, and even explosions are other occurrences encountered. In fact modern racing boats are designed to self-destruct in the event of a crash in order to lessen the impact on the occupants, much like modern automotive designs. Impact zones and energy-absorbing construction techniques are doing much to reduce the frequency of serious driver injuries.

Prepared for disaster

Because the boats are prone to accidents, many occupants use a five-point harness system for protection. But some crews prefer not using safety harnesses in order to be thrown clear of the hull if they do crash—the greatest fear is being held underwater and drowned in the event of an accident.

Unlike most extreme sports, powerboat racing is expensive, and so crews rely on sponsors to buy signage on their hulls in order to offset the financial burden. Powerboats require a lot of time in testing designs and engines to insure competitiveness, further adding to the cost of racing. Many top teams spend well in excess of $1.5 million (£1 million) annually to be competitive and race.

The nature of powerboat racing requires participants to constantly test and reevaluate current technologies. As these technologies are advanced, it is conceivable that something will happen to enhance the safety of racing. However, it is unlikely that traveling at speed on the water will ever be considered a thrill that anyone but an extreme enthusiast will enjoy.

Cat hull-powerboats require much less horsepower than the single V-hull designs.

Round the World

The Trophée Jules Verne

When Jules Verne penned his classic novel *Around the World in 80 Days* in the late nineteenth century, he relied heavily on his imagination to propel hero Phileas Fogg and trusty servant Passepartout in their land, sea, and air circumnavigation of earth. Today, that imagination is embodied in the Trophée Jules Verne, a crewed non-stop race around the world. While Fogg and Passepartout traveled by ship for a fraction of their voyage, this race is entirely waterborne.

(Above and right) The *Commodore Explorer*, captained by Frenchman Bruno Peyron, in 1993 became the first sailing vessel to circumnavigate the globe by water in less than 80 days.

Yacht Racing

THE RACE BEGAN in the fall of 1993, when a French and a New Zealand entry passed an imaginary line stretching across the western approaches to the English Channel, which is also where they would be required to finish. The two multihulls streaked down the Atlantic Ocean until, somewhere south of Cape Town, South Africa, the New Zealand entry hit a submerged object. One of its hulls damaged, the crew were forced to life-saving measures to keep the catamaran afloat. They eventually made port under their own power, to return a year later to play an important role in the development of this young race.

As the New Zealanders limped toward South Africa, the Frenchmen pressed on. A six-man crew led by world record-holder Bruno Peyron, and including American specialist Cam Lewis, were sailing a huge and powerful catamaran, *Commodore Explorer*. The craft measured 88 feet (27m).

Catamarans are among the fastest type of sailboat in the world. With their hulls spread so far apart and the main power unit, the mast and mainsail, placed in between those hulls, catamarans can leverage the wind, sailing nearly twice as fast as the windspeed in a variety of wind and sea conditions.

Success

Harnessing and controlling speed, both windspeed and boatspeed, is a problem with multihulls, and is most problematic in the winds and waves of the Southern Ocean. With no land mass to slow the prevailing currents of

wind and water, the Southern Ocean, generally considered the body of water below latitude 50°S, is the most treacherous body of water on the planet. Wave heights topping 50 feet (15m) and windspeeds in excess of 75 mph (120 kph) can develop instantly, bringing with them hail, sleet, or blinding snowstorms.

With no visibility, radar is heavily relied on to see icebergs that could sink a boat with just a glancing blow. Most bergs are the size of a New York City street block, so the electronic seeing eye usually picks them up easily. Not so visible, however, are "growlers," large chunks of ice that break off the bergs. Growlers are typically half-submerged and commonly jut out underwater. They are so sharp that they can easily puncture the composite hulls of today's ocean racing sailboats.

The Frenchmen survived the trials and tribulations of a circumnavigation. They survived collisions with whales, they survived hurricanes, they survived hull damage, they survived hitting submerged logs, and they rewarded themselves by becoming the first sailing vessel to circumnavigate the globe by water in less than 80 days. They covered 27,372 miles (44,041 km) in 79 days, 6 hours, 15 minutes and 56 seconds, a total of 1,902 consecutive hours at sea.

Their record would stand for only a year, though. The New Zealanders returned, led by two of the more famous modern circum-

navigators, and crushed *Commodore Explorer*'s record. Skippers Peter Blake, winner of the Whitbread Round the World Race, and Robin Knox-Johnston, the first man to single-handedly circumnavigate the globe non-stop, created a team full of experience and commonsense.

An extreme legend

They used the experience gained in their previous, aborted attempt to modify their catamaran. They increased its overall length to 92 feet (28m), modified the hull shape, and changed the rig configuration. The new and improved craft then took them and a crew of five around the world in a record time of 74 days, 22 hours, 17 minutes and 22 seconds, a record which still stands.

They sailed almost 1,000 miles less than the original record-setters because they went much deeper into the Southern Ocean, below latitude 60°S, taking advantage of the earth's natural curvature to sail less distance, and set 12 world records along the way. Their determination to risk their lives and their boat in order to establish a new level of global sailing performance is the stuff of extreme sailing legend, and a feat that will be difficult to better.

The *Commodore Explorer*'s arrival at the finishing line was greeted with a spectacular example of the effectiveness of flares at sea.

Bruno Peyron (right) congratulates Peter Blake (left) and Robin Knox-Johnston after they shattered his record by almost 5 days in 1994.

The Whitbread Race

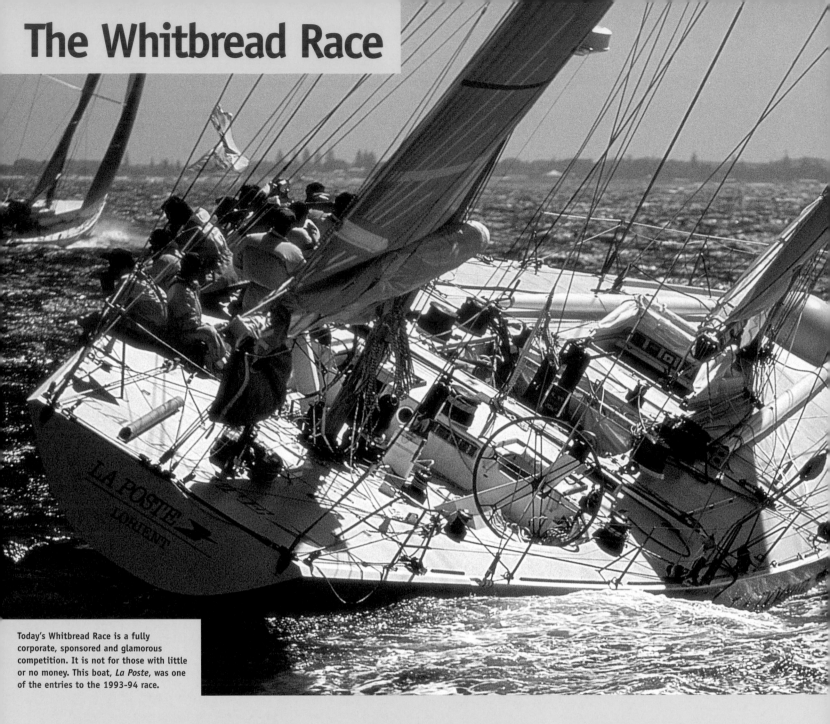

Today's Whitbread Race is a fully corporate, sponsored and glamorous competition. It is not for those with little or no money. This boat, *La Poste*, was one of the entries to the 1993-94 race.

Offshore sailboat racing has two distinct disciplines. At one end of the spectrum is singlehanded sailing, where a solitary skipper puts his sailing knowledge, navigational expertise, will—even his life—on the line. At the other is crewed sailing, where crews between 12–20 sailors, specializing in particular tasks, rely upon one another as a team in the quest for victory.

AMONG THE GREATEST RACES in the world in crewed racing is the Whitbread Round the World Race. Dubbed the "ultimate ocean race," it was the first of its kind, with origins dating back to 1973.

Four years earlier, in 1969, Englishman Robin Knox-Johnston had won the Golden Globe Race, and was the first to singlehandedly circumnavigate the globe non-stop. He was one of eight to start the challenge sponsored by London newspaper *The Sunday Times*, but the only sailor to finish. The event was considered more a challenge than a race because competitors were allowed to begin their voyage at any time between June and October of 1968.

Knox-Johnston's accomplishment started a frenzy of activity to organize the first official round the world race for fully-crewed sailboats. Watching with keen interest were the British navy and army, who were in the process of obtaining several 55-foot (17m) boats for adventure training. When rivals couldn't get a race organized by April 1972, the British navy forged ahead with the Whitbread, and in September 1973 a legend was born.

Lives lost

The first competition was historic for many reasons: it was the first, crewed, circum-navigational race of its kind; it was the first race of its kind to send crews into the treacherous waters known as the Roaring Forties and Screaming Fifties—the Southern Ocean; and it resulted in the fastest, crewed circumnavigation of its time.

The race—the Southern Ocean in particular—proved even more challenging than the competitors had imagined. Leg two of the four-legged course took the fleet of 17 entrants from Cape Town, South Africa, to Sydney, Australia; and leg three went from Sydney to Rio de Janeiro, Brazil. Not only were these extremely long distances to sail, but they covered the Southern Ocean, the great expanse of water separating the six inhabited continents from the seventh, Antarctica. Unimpeded by land, storm systems sweep across these deep southern latitudes, gaining so much force that they become life threatening.

The *Reebok*'s name reflects how important sponsorship has become to the survival of the Whitbread.

Three lives were lost in the Southern Ocean, all the result of crew members falling overboard. One sailor was presumably unconscious when a sheet flung him over. Another was swept off the deck during a sail change, when a huge breaking wave hit the boat. The third man was lost as he went forward for a sail change, apparently lost his footing and fell overboard. Down below on the vessels, crews worked frantically to keep water out of the boats—an almost impossible task when you're sailing at latitude 60°S for two weeks at a time.

Today, the Whitbread Race is a fully corporate, sponsored, and highly glamorous competition. The event occurs every fourth year beginning in the fall, and finishes in the spring, some six months later. Whereas the first race in 1973/74 was largely a corinthian effort, today some skippers can earn as much as $150,000 (£100,000) to lead a corporation's entry. There are more legs for the next race than there were in the original, nine as opposed to four, and the boats are drastically different.

Mental peak

Unlike the crews of the original Whitbread, their counterparts today are as much concerned with how to get water into the boat as they are with keeping it out. The introduction of water-ballast systems (very common among the singlehanded spectrum) is a feature on the new Whitbread 60 class of boats, 60-footers (18m) capable of reaching speeds nearly three times as great in the Southern Ocean as the 1973-74 pioneers were able to.

The Whitbread incorporates a vast array of challenges ranging from surviving powerful storms, to exhaustion, and even continuing after crew deaths. The crews are aware that they too could be lost at sea, that their yachts may not return, and that—at the very least—they will be required to perform at their physical and mental peaks for months with only a few onshore breaks. This is team sailboat racing at its most extreme.

The BOC Challenge and the Vendée Globe

Singlehanded racing is the aquatic version of marathon running, where the skipper has to draw from resources deep within himself for the endurance and stamina necessary to sail 30 days or more alone at sea. Unlike the marathon runner, whose most important equipment is his shoes, a singlehanded sailor's equipment is a sailboat often as large as 60 feet (18m) and its accompanying systems—and it all has to be maintained continuously.

(Above) Frenchman, Philippe Poupon in charge of his boat *Fleury Michon X* in the Vendée Globe race in 1989-90, and (below) taking a few moments to reflect on the task ahead of him.

JOSHUA SLOCUM is considered the grandfather of singlehanded sailors. Between 1895 and 1898, Slocum singlehandedly circumnavigated the globe in a wooden boat, making several stops along the way. Another 69 years elapsed before Francis Chichester completed a one-stop, singlehanded circumnavigation. Then, in 1969, Robin Knox-Johnston completed the first non-stop, singlehanded circumnavigation to win the Golden Globe Challenge.

Founded in 1982, the BOC Challenge is one of two singlehanded circumnavigation races. Its rival—and considered more difficult by some—is the Vendée Globe race. Instituted in 1989, the Vendée Globe is distinguished by its simpleness and extremeness; it is an all-out sprint departing and finishing in France whose basic requirements are leaving Antarctica to starboard and returning unassisted. With no stops or assistance allowed in the global race, sailors must learn to fix anything that breaks on their boat, or learn to live without

Full-rigged sailing boats in action, like the *Cacharel* pictured below, are an obvious reminder of why people love the challenge of the sea.

it. Their will must be strong enough to stitch themselves together after suffering a severe laceration in a knockdown, and then go on deck and stitch the sail together that ripped in the same accident.

Carbon fiber

The BOC has more stature worldwide because it led to a new generation of singlehanded sailors, as well as boats. Many speed-enhancing features now key to today's singlehanded sailor were developed and refined in the heat of BOC competition—water ballast systems, autopilots, twin rudders, and the use of carbon fiber as a construction material in the hull and masts.

Skipper preparation for either race is as important as boat preparation. Pre-race rest is crucial, since solo sailing skippers get very little sleep. A common routine sees many skippers catnap for 30 to 40 minutes when they become tired. But in a span of 24 hours, they are lucky if they get six such naps. Constant vigilance is the name of this game.

In terms of pushing the limits of individual performance, both mentally and physically, singlehanded around the world yacht racing is one of the most challenging sports in terms of danger and time spent at risk. Of course those that take part in the races will tell you it is for the love of being on the water that they do it.

Scuba Diving

The mysteries of the sea have driven many to brave the ocean depths to experience first-hand what it feels like to live beneath the water's surface. Those who pioneered modern scuba did so at great risk—our bodies were not meant to breathe under water, nor were they meant to breathe under the pressure of millions of pounds of liquid. As you go deeper into the sea, your body is no longer able to use the air you breathe as effectively as above the surface. As a result, hundreds of diving fatalities occur each year.

MAN'S SEARCH for a means to breathe underwater can be traced back to the ancient Romans, when early divers used a floatation device to support airhoses attached to leather helmets to provide oxygen.

It was not until 1819 that deep-sea diving became a practical reality, when German inventor Augustus Siebein developed the bulky brass dive helmet linked to an air compressor back on the ship.

Nearly 130 years later, famous marine biologist Jacques Cousteau invented the aqualung together with fellow pioneer Emil Gagnan. The aqualung finally released divers from the restraints of air hoses and compressors and allowed them to swim freely through the water. The aqualung is unquestionably the most important invention in modern diving.

Since the aqualung's introduction, scuba (self contained underwater breathing apparatus) has grown into an incredibly popular sport enjoyed by pleasure seekers, treasure hunters, researchers, and sportsmen globally. However, despite its popularity, scuba diving remains a dangerous sport that

Despite encounters with a white tip shark such as this, human error is the likeliest source of danger for the scuba diver.

requires an in-depth knowledge of the effects extreme pressure can have on the body: how a diver absorbs air under these changing conditions, and a broad understanding of how to deal appropriately with the effects of pressure-breathing if accidents are to be avoided. One study of diving fatalities has revealed that the greatest danger lies not with the equipment but with the diver—almost all fatalities are due to human error.

Under pressure

There are other hazards. Hypothermia is a condition caused by the lowering of the body's core temperature, which can be fatal if prolonged. Sharp coral and rocks can cause injury, and strong underwater currents can separate dive partners (it's always advisable to dive in pairs at least) or, worse, sweep divers

Wreck diving, while dangerous, has always held a mysterious appeal for scuba divers.

Sharp coral and strong currents can seriously injure an inexperienced diver.

Technological developments, like this underwater scooter, have assisted divers in pushing the limits of their chosen extreme sport.

away from their support boat. Perhaps the most universally feared hazard is an encounter with a large shark or group of sharks. Smaller sharks can be docile if left alone, but they are never to be trusted. Larger sharks, such as tiger or great white sharks, are perpetually seeking food, and anything that swims is usually fair game.

Maladies associated with diving stem from how the body processes the air stored under pressure in the diver's tanks. As a diver swims deeper the body has to cope with increasing levels of pressure, measured in atmospheres. One "atmosphere" is the equivalent of the pressure exerted on the body at sea level, two atmospheres is double the pressure, and so on. As atmospheres increase, the pressure forces greater levels of breathed air into the bloodstream as gases. Under controlled conditions at relatively shallow depths, this is not a problem until the diver surfaces. As the diver ascends, these gases—most notably nitrogen—start escaping from the bloodstream. The ascent must be controlled and slow enough to allow the gases to be released through normal exhalation through the diver's lungs. If the diver ascends too quickly, the gases can bubble out into the body tissue, causing muscular pain and bodily damage. It's a bit like the effect you see when you open a can or bottle of pressurized carbonated soda.

The results can be deadly, causing the body to curl up and convulse spastically—hence the name of "bends" for the condition. Non-fatal repercussions of the bends include coma, neurological disorders, and intense abdominal pain. Nitrogen—the main component of divers' compressed air—can have other side effect. One of the most alarming is "nitrogen narcosis." It is more common on deeper dives, where the increased pressure forces more nitrogen into the bloodstream, and takes the form of drowsiness—potentially lethal under water.

Getting technical

A decompression chamber—a large tank that can compress the air inside to several atmospheres—is commonly found on vessels used as dive-support stations. Divers experiencing the bends are placed inside the decompression chamber and then quickly "returned" to the appropriate atmospheric pressure they were under in the water before the too-rapid ascent began. This allows the diver to complete the necessary decompression time and can halt the effects of the bends.

Diving using normal air mixtures—equivalent to the air we breathe every day—limits the depth and duration of dives. The deeper the dive, the less amount of time can be spent at the maximum depth. Knowing what the maximum lengths of time are for each depth is critical for diver safety.

Divers wanting to go deeper and stay down longer have to use different mixtures of air. Because of the extra requirements and the greater complexity of the process, deep dives are referred to as "technical" dives. Technical divers generally use enriched air such as "nitrox," a mixture with dramatically elevated amounts of oxygen. The use of enriched air mixtures is not recommended to any but the most experienced and well-trained of divers—Russian roulette is probably safer than technical diving without the required training and experience. A further system, called "rebreathing," utilizes a high-tech method of removing oxygen from exhaled air and recycling it for reuse.

Deep technical diving is the extreme end of scuba. Deep divers must have a rock solid understanding of the physiology and psychology of diving as well as strong stress-management skills. Planning each dive is imperative so that decompression occurs at the proper rate and accidents are avoided.

Get trained—and live

The current record for deep diving using a non-enriched mixture was unofficially established in 1994 by Dr. Dan Manion, who dived to 506 feet (290m) and lost consciousness during his ascent. The record for deep diving using a

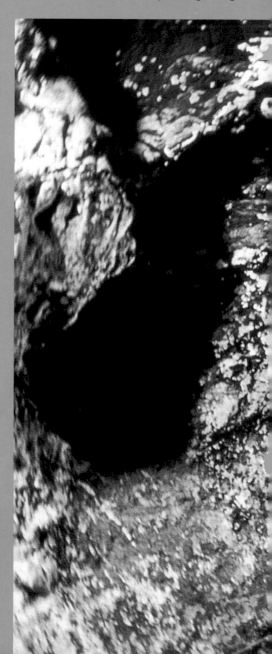

combination of rebreathing and mixed gases was made the same year by two technical divers in Zacaton, Mexico, the world's deepest underwater cave system. Jim Bowden and Sheck Exley attempted to descend to 1,000 feet (305m). Bowden reached 925 feet before returning to the surface. Exley disappeared at around 906 feet, and his fate is unknown.

Scuba is a dangerous sport, even for those seeking to dive for pleasure. Only those with enough training should dive. Even simple holiday excursions can result in tragedy. Extreme diving and depth record-setting is absolutely not recommended to anyone but the most expert divers, and even they are placing themselves at tremendous risk. Surely the depth record will be broken at some point, but almost as certain is that lives will be lost in the process.

Encounters with the inhabitants of the sea are not always as amicable as with these Bottlenose dolphins in the Caribbean Sea.

Exploring underwater cave systems, like the Devil's Eye off the Florida coast is one of the more dangerous aspects of scuba diving.

Snorkeling

Snorkeling is a pleasureable way to swim gently along the beach or in clear waters where fish and reefs are in view. The detail from the surface, or up close in the shallow areas, is what most swimmers equate with snorkeling. However there is a darker, deeper, and extreme type of snorkeling that few would consider doing without a tank, if at all.

BLUE WATER HUNTERS are a combination of freediver and spearfisher, and swim down slowly into the water, careful not to disturb any of the larger, and tastier, inhabitants. The diver must maintain a state of calm and heightened awareness in order to get a glimpse of the big fish they seek to catch. Quiet, methodical movements are the only way extreme snorkelers will avoid scaring their prey.

Better divers release the seal around their snorkels and fill their mouths with water to prevent any air bubbles from alerting fish to their presence. They must constantly swivel around 180 degrees to

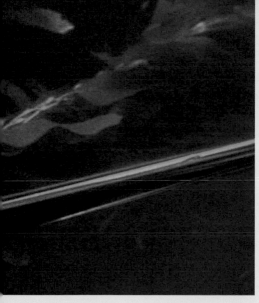

stay prepared for approaching fish, and the occasional shark. Incredible focus is required to notice oncoming fish and potentially unfriendly sealife in the distance before being seen, giving enough time to prepare for the shot. Divers keep a lookout for schools of bait fish that draw larger predators, and hope for "the big one" to show up.

Divers can effectively lure fish closer by staying horizontal and looking head on as they approach. If the fish feel the diver is as small as his profile, they may become curious and seek a closer look. Other methods of luring fish include making croaking noises and setting bait or artificial lures.

Divers typically rise to the surface for around 45 seconds before submerging again, and try to stay down as long as possible, usually 60 seconds or more. They try to position themselves for optimum shooting when a fish is in the area. The best angle for a shot is downward and around 10–15 feet (3–4.5m) away. Quiet divers can blend into their environment and get close enough to be in range.

Divers carry an assortment of gear on each trip out, including a wetsuit, snorkel and mask, fins, and a hand spear or spear gun. Additional equipment includes a weightbelt, dive knife, gear bag, and back-up items. A typical spear gun measures around 5–6 feet (1.5–1.8m) in length using 6-foot spears made from stainless steel. The butt end of the gun is weighted to afford the diver better balance and more control over the gun, as well as additional ballast to help them stay submerged. The ballast consists of lead shot which can be added or removed if needed.

(Left) A state of calm mixed with heightened awareness separates the good blue water hunter from the rest. (Below) This huge Spanish mackerel speaks volumes about this hunter's abilities.

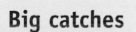

169

Big catches

Extreme snorkelers do not generally seek out small prey, but are in search of larger stuff, in the 200–500 lb (90–270 kg) category. Blue- and yellow-fin tuna, black marlin, and other larger game fish separate this style of spear fishing from the tamer stuff. Many divers can tell stories of landing huge fish, only to be nearly drowned in the tow that ensued. It is therefore highly critical that the diver hit the target in the right spot and score a quick kill. Aside from the risk of a long battle while being towed, there is the very real risk of a physical confrontation with their catch, which can be a life or death struggle. Consider a 500 lb marlin coming full speed with its spear shaped nose pointed at you.

The sport is certainly not for the tame. It does, however, provide a new perspective on a sport that is relatively safe and rarely considered extreme.

Speed Sailing

Speed has been a quest of sailing pioneers for as long as there have been sailing vessels. In early times, speed meant sailors could travel farther to catch bigger and better quantities of fish. Speed allowed explorers to gain access to new frontiers before supplies dwindled and starvation ensued. As warriors sought control of the seas, speed offered aggressors the opportunity of a swift attack, and gave those seeking escape the chance to elude their demise. Today, the quest for speed is all about establishing new levels of performance and securing a spot in the record books.

In the 1980s the Trifoiler smashed all previous speed sailing records. But its efficiency was limited by its design.

SPEED SAILING FOR SPORT has brought with it most of the current high-technology equipment and space-age materials now common in everyday sailing. Sailing faster requires lighter watercraft that hardly resemble the sailboats of even a decade ago— the vessel currently holding the speed sailing record cannot be turned, and can only sail in one direction! Speed sailing is a highly specialized sport requiring highly specialized designs. The only goal is to accelerate within a straight, closed course, and pass through a

Yellow Pages

ENDEAVOUR

RONSTAN & BOLE COLE
S T R O & CLUBMARINE
HONDA & SP Systems
ANL & swan HARDWARE

section of that course at maximum velocity in hope of recording a new speed record. To break the record in practice is only momentarily satisfying, as no speed is official without being recorded at a sanctioned event site, with official timekeepers present. So the object is to design a boat that can break records on any given day in any reasonable breeze—official events and perfect conditions do not always coincide.

For years the record books were filled with catamarans, and every successful attempt merely edged out the previous record. Catamarans are sailboats with two slender hulls that slice through the water, offering little resistance other than the inescapable surface tension between their hulls and the water. Going faster meant minimizing the amount of hull surface that contacted the water and maximizing the amount of horsepower the sails could generate. This meant huge rigs carrying tremendous sails on hulls that barely sustained the loads placed on them. This led to terribly overpowered sailboats that self-destructed under the forces they generated more often then they would set records.

Trifoils

In the Eighties, the records established by catamarans were suddenly destroyed by tiny, specially designed sailboards which were hardly in contact with the water at speed and required sails small enough that they could be supported by the sailor. Sailboards owned the world speed record for nearly a decade.

The Yellow Pages-sponsored craft *Endeavour* (below and opposite) is a speed record-specific design. The crew sit in a tiny compartment at the end of one of its "wings".

Then in 1992 a new and radical sailing hydrofoil shattered the record by traveling at 50.02 knots on an official course at the French Trench outside of Calais, France. The Trifoiler designed by Californian Greg Ketterman was much smaller and lighter than previous record setters, with the obvious exception of sailboards. The Trench is famous for its strong sideways winds and narrow, protected waters that ensure a nearly perfect flat water surface. The Trifoiler reduced speed-limiting surface to a only a small fraction of what had been previously reached during years of effort.

This record-setting design did have a limiting factor, and that was the efficiency of the wing-like foils that lift the boat out of the water at speed. These create speed-limiting drag at top end of their performance,

making it impossible for them to travel faster. An Australian design dubbed "Yellow Pages," named after the craft's sponsor, used a design similar in appearance to Ketterman's Trifoiler, however rather than using hydrofoils Yellow Pages used small skis to ride on. This both greatly reduced the surface tension that earlier catamaran designs suffered and eliminated the top-end performance limits of the Trifoiler's.

Quest for speed

Yellow Pages was a speed-record-specific design incapable of turning or sailing in more than one direction. But it was fast enough to edge out the Trifoiler for top spot in the record books. Because it used skis to ride on, it was a step back in the direction of the

speed record-setting sailboards. But, because it used a large sail held up by stays (wires), it could carry far more sail area than any sailboard, and therefore had a tremendous horsepower advantage.

The quest for the World Speed Sailing record continues. Somewhere, now, there is a designer working hard to redefine the limits of wind-driven speed on water. Given that land-sailing vehicles are capable of exceeding 100 mph (160 kph), it is surely only a matter of time before sailboats will reach such speeds. When that occurs the way we travel over water will be forever changed. This is bound to expand the distances sailing vessels can cover, since unlike land sailcraft which are limited by the terrain available to cover, speed sailcraft will have an endless supply of water, and the distances traveled will be limited only by their design's ability to deal with a variety of surface conditions.

Surfing

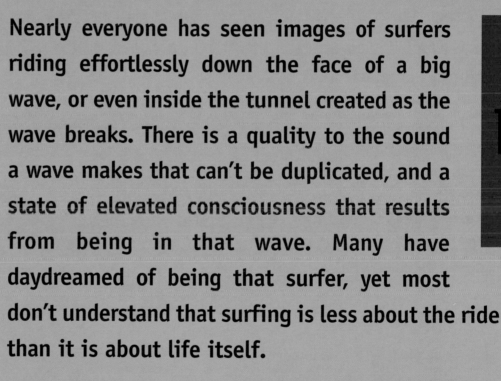

Nearly everyone has seen images of surfers riding effortlessly down the face of a big wave, or even inside the tunnel created as the wave breaks. There is a quality to the sound a wave makes that can't be duplicated, and a state of elevated consciousness that results from being in that wave. Many have daydreamed of being that surfer, yet most don't understand that surfing is less about the ride than it is about life itself.

ASK ANY SURFER to explain what it feels like to surf and they will tell you to try it for yourself, since as one surfer eloquently stated, "trying to explain surfing to a non-surfer is like trying to explain sex to a virgin." There is something mystical about the entire process of surfing, something that can only be experienced.

Each wave at every surf spot is as different from the last as one snowflake is from another. Consider that each wave has traveled hundreds or thousands of miles to get to the shore, and has met countless forces that ultimately determine how it will break, and when. Every swell contains a series of waves which vary in speed, angle of approach, and size. In that sense surfing is much like life, with a different twist and turn around each corner, whether it is a personality or a circumstance one is dealing with, each is unique and requires a unique response. As in surfing, the proper response means harmony, and the wrong response can be devastating.

Hawaiian, Laird Hamilton (right), leads American Pete Cabrina down this huge Hawaiian wave.

The waves off the coast of Victoria, Australia, offer some of the best surfing anywhere in the world.

Surfing began centuries ago in the Pacific Island cultures where its roots can be traced to the beginnings of Polynesian society. By the seventeenth and eighteenth centuries, surfing was a widely accepted aspect of both the ruling and working classes in Hawaii. Surfing was to these people a part of their secular lives, replete with surfing gods, sacred rituals, and a strong set of social norms all linked to surfing.

Early Hawaiians took their surfing very seriously. Hawaiian chiefs could declare any of their favorite surfing spots "Kapu," meaning they were off limits to all but the

chief and his friends. Chiefs would direct their subjects to bring only the finest wood from the cold highland regions of the island. The best craftsmen would be entrusted with shaping the chief's board from the wood, often from the prized koa or the wiliwili tree. Commoners would ride boards of much less exotic wood. Yet regardless of the value of the surfboard, it was always treated with respect. A proper surfbuilding ritual was always performed out of respect for the surf gods so as to provide the owner with good waves and the safety of being protected from harm.

Surfer forefathers

Reports of surfing were first described to the civilized world by Lieutenant James King of the British Royal Navy in 1779. He remarked that he'd seen Hawaiians surfing massive "boomers" at Kealakekua Bay. In typical fashion of the self righteous explorers of the period, he described surfing as "most perilous and extraordinary, altogether astonishing and scarcely to be credited."

Surfing, of course, continued despite the lieutenant's comments and eventually over 150 years later, under the leadership of legendary Duke Kahanamoku, grew to become the international force in watersports it is today. Duke was the first recognized star of the surfing community. He was so famous that Hollywood stars flocked to Hawaii to meet and be photographed with him.

Duke is credited with being the founding father of modern surfing, and organized the first surf club in the world, the Hui Nalu. "Da Hui" still thrives today and is known throughout the world. Its membership consists of the biggest names in the surfing world, past and present, and loyalty among its members is extremely strong. Other notable surf clubs formed by influential Hawaiians include the Outrigger Club, and the Healani.

Surfing reached California in the Fifties where it spawned a cultural revolution, inspiring the popularity of the beach lifestyle that was reflected in the surf music of Dick Dale and the Beach Boys. Surf films glorifying the Hawaiian and Californian surf culture became wildly popular at the same time. Amazingly, though, some of the very first surf movies were produced by Thomas Edison, who filmed surfers at Honolulu's famed Waikiki Beach in 1898.

Big surf summer

Surf movies gained a wider audience with the work of pioneers like Bruce Brown, who captured the authentic surfing scene with his first feature film, *The Big Surf*, in 1943. His most notable film was *The Endless Summer*, which followed a few nomadic surfers on a quest for the perfect wave. Its sequel, *The Endless Summer II*, released in 1994, has inspired an international following similar to

Pete Cabrina is one of the leading toe-in surfers who has crossed from pro boardsailing.

that of his first film. Surf movies are available today by a host of film-makers, and are widely accessible on video.

Making big waves

Modern surfing has progressed tremendously since the days of massive wooden boards ridden by the pioneers of surfing in Hawaii and the Polynesian islands. Today's surfboards vary enormously in size and shape. Professional surfers own a "quiver" (collection) of different boards designed to perform in all ranges of surf conditions. Shorter boards in lengths of 5–7 feet (1.5–2m) are used primarily in smaller waves for maneuverability and work well with the shape of the faces on smaller waves.

Short boards have been credited for many of today's freestyle tricks. These moves are unlike any seen in the history of surfing, with many taking inspiration from what has been done in skateboarding. Riders are getting their boards out of the water like a skateboarder in a half-pipe, doing 360-degree spins, rail grabs, and other highly technical tricks that have come to redefine modern surfing. Freestyle surfing pioneers like Matt Archbold and Christian Fletcher have had a major impact on the freestyle movement as leaders of the new art.

Bruce Ellis of Australia, demonstrates the strength of the Hawaiian surf.

"Gun" surfboards of between 8–11 feet (2.4–3.4m) are used for speed and bigger waves. Their longer profiles give added edge holding in big surf where speeds are considerably greater than in lesser conditions. Big-wave surfing is also experiencing a renaissance, with new and hazardous spots like Mavericks in Northern California competing for attention with some of the more recognizable big-wave locations like Pipeline on the North Shore of Oahu. Mavericks gained international recognition for its extreme conditions when surf star Mark Foo lost his life after being engulfed by one of Mavericks's moderate-sized waves. What makes Mavericks especially dangerous is the jagged rocks and caves beneath the surface that surfers get sucked into after wiping out.

Dinosaur returns

"Longboards" are now making a comeback in surfing after years of being thought second class to the newer short surfboards. For many years, longboards have been considered to be made for "old men" and "kooks" (surfer lingo for novices with no skills and even less

178

America's Ross Williams in classic surfing action.

intelligence). Now surfers are getting a new, almost nostalgic, respect for longboards and those who ride them, at least those who really know how to ride them.

The newest entrants to the surfboard world are the "tow-in" boards used to surf the biggest and scariest waves in the world. The sport was pioneered by Hawaiian surfing legend Gerry Lopez and a crew of surfers turned pro boardsailors, turned surfers, led by native Hawaiian Laird Hamilton. Hamilton and other notables, including Dave Kalama, Mike Waltz, Peter Cabrina, Mark Angulo, and Rush Randall, all crossed over from surfing into the world of pro boardsailing where they learned the control advantages that footstraps offered.

Into deep water

This group began experimenting with short and narrow speed board designs that could be towed behind a Jet Ski, much like waterskis. They found that by being towed, they could let go of the tow line while in large waves, and ride them even before they began to crest and break. This, they discovered, enabled them to get dropped into waves that could never have been ridden before, either because they were too long a paddle from shore, or because they were simply too dangerous to attempt to ride the old fashioned way. These surfers have ridden waves that without a doubt are

The spectacular 'Jaws' wave off Maui, Hawaii, can kill a surfer who suffers a bad wipeout.

Laird Hamilton is continually on the quest for establishing new boundaries of performance for big wave surfers.

the largest ever successfully negotiated by any surfers in the world.

Ride the big wave

The most famous of the tow-in spots is a particularly dangerous reef, aptly named "Jaws." The mushroom-shaped reef, located "somewhere" in the Hawaiian Islands, creates a wave that jumps up and breaks in a crescent shape. The wave heights in a big swell easily exceed 50 feet (15m) and are certainly capable of killing anyone unfortunate enough to get caught in a bad wipeout. The waves are so powerful that it is not uncommon for them to hold a surfer down

for 60 seconds or more in a wipeout. Surfers are reportedly experimenting with miniature tanks to provide much needed air in the event of a deadly hold down.

Big-wave and tow-in surfing appear to be the future of modern surfing. Both can certainly be considered extreme because they epitomize the common theme among extreme sports—the quest for establishing new boundaries of performance. It is hard to visualize what direction they will point surfing in, and even harder to imagine that surfing will continue to progress to riding bigger and bigger waves without losing a few top athletes to the forces of nature.

Trifoiling

The Trifoiler is an excellent example of how extreme sports and the yearning for technological advances to increase performance can change an entire category of sport.

JUST A FEW SHORT YEARS AGO the speed-sailing community was in awe of new speed records that were being set by specialized windsurfers breaking into the mid-40-knot (46 mph, 74 kph) speed range. Surely it would be these boards that would redefine speed sailing. However, a mechanical engineer named Greg Ketterman was at the time experimenting with the concept of a speed sailboat that progressed on hydrofoils, a concept that may well change the future of sailing.

Ketterman, widely known for his work on the Stars and Stripes Catamaran used in 1987 to beat New Zealand's enormous monohull and retain the America's Cup, first began playing with radio-controlled versions of a hydrofoiled sailboat around 1980. California speed sailor and yacht racer Russell Long commissioned Ketterman to build him a full size version of the hydrofoil design for a speed record attempt in 1989. He successfully set a new Class A speed record in 1992 at an amazing 50.08 knots at Saint Marie de la Mer, also known as "The French Trench." The site, widely recognized as the premier speed-sailing site in the world, is a long and narrow channel of water where prevailing winds are strong yet leave the water's surface almost unaffected.

The concept of creating a sailboat that could ride on a hydrofoil was not new. What was keeping designers from success was the

nature of the hydrofoil wings. Hydrofoils are essentially like airplane wings that have been optimized to perform in water. Therefore, like an airplane wing, they generate lift, and must be controlled so that they do not seek to go straight upward. Airplanes use steering devices built into their wings which allow the pilot to determine the amount of lift they generate and to maintain a level path if desired.

Riding high

Airplanes have a distinct advantage over hydrofoils, because they need to travel through the same medium their wings do. The whole concept about hydrofoils is to get the boat out of the water, thereby nearly

eliminating hydrodynamic resistance that the hulls create, and delivering virtually limitless speed potential. To be successful, a hydrofoil needs to ride high enough to get the boat out of the water and—since they only work in the water—low enough to stay submerged. Therefore, unlike airplanes, hydrofoil wings have a limited margin of error and must maintain a course that can only vary within inches to be effective.

Powerboat designers figured how to make hydrofoils work decades ago. The big problems occur with the addition of sails, because the force a sail generates is high above the boat, and constantly working to push the boat over onto its side. This

tendency for sailboats to tip is what held back designers for years.

Ketterman invented a new approach to keeping the foils in the water. He added a "sensor" to the foil design that could read the pitch of the foil (whether it was heading up, down, or level) and correct it to maintain a level track. The addition of the sensor was the breakthrough that made hydrofoil sailing a possibility. The sensor pushes the foil down if it's heading up, and pulls the foil up if it's heading down. The result is that the foil constantly corrects itself, keeping the hulls out of the water and the foils in.

The 20-foot (6m) Trifoiler design positions two J-shaped foils beneath its two sails in front of the boat's bobsled-like cockpit. The sails are positioned bi-plane style, maximizing the sail area and minimizing the sail's propensity to "heel" (tip) the boat out of its most efficient, flat stance. The Trifoiler is lifted from behind by a T-shaped foil on the bottom of the "rudder" (steering foil). The resulting triangular stance is highly stable and maneuverable. Because the foils are firmly "locked" into the water, the boat can turn quickly, pulling as much as 2 gees of lateral acceleration in a turn without sliding sideways, much like a toy slot-car on its track.

User friendly

Top speed on a Trifoiler is over 50 mph (80 kph), with only the efficiency of today's foil designs keeping it from going faster. In fact at top speed, the low pressure on the top of the foil resulting from the foil's lift, actually boils the water, causing speed-limiting drag. Ketterman is working on new foil designs that will allow for higher speeds.

The Trifoiler design is so stable and user friendly that Ketterman's Trifoiler was recently purchased by Hobie Corporation (makers of the famous Hobie Catamarans) and is now available to anyone wishing to sail as fast as possible. The boats are easy enough to handle for even novice sailors to sail.

The Trifoiler design will certainly gain popularity over the next several years. Today, they simply can't make them fast enough. As the technology improves, larger and faster versions are sure to be developed. In the meantime, look for these extreme sailboats to show up soon wherever there is wind and water.

Wakeboarding

Wakeboarding is a relatively new extreme sport. Its heritage can be linked to waterskiing, surfing, windsurfing, skateboarding, and snowboarding, and it is quickly redefining how we look at boat-towed sports.

THE CONCEPT OF TOWING a surfboard behind either a boat in the water or a car on the beach on waveless days is as old as modern surfing. The need to ride on a board drives many "sideways" sports enthusiasts to try whatever they need to get out and ride on their boards. That's how skateboarding began, and later windsurfing and snowboarding. For decades, if there was no surf, surfers were known to grab a line and get pulled by a boat or even by a truck running onshore. This was no easy trick, since this was not the intended purpose of a surfboard. Strong surfers could pull it off and get some turns in on a flat day.

In 1985, San Diego surfer Tony Finn created and developed a waterski/surfboard he called the Skurfer. The Skurfer was narrower than a surfboard and riders could do snowboard-like turns behind their boats. Soon, with the addition of footstraps, skurfers were riding their boards and performing many of the same maneuvers that snowboarders were doing. That same year, Texas surfer Jimmy Redmond added footstraps to another early wakeboard design.

The early skurfers pushed hard and began getting big air and pulling off dynamic moves, however the appeal didn't grow far outside of the community of strong skiers because the Skurfer's narrow and highly buoyant design made it difficult to master. In 1990 waterski pioneer Hugh O'Brien gathered together many top surfers to create a board design that had many of the performance characteristics of a good surfboard.

The "Hyperlite" design that was created had neutral buoyancy, and was compression-molded like the waterskis O'Brien's H.O. Sports company was mass-producing. The neutral buoyancy design and thin profile rails (edges of the board) allowed the Hyperlite design to carve shorter, slalom-like turns than the Skurfer. The design also made getting up and mastering the board easier, growing the appeal of what would be called the wakeboard.

Doing the grind

Indents called "phasers" were added to help break up the water flow under the board, making the board feel "looser" (less stuck to the water) and making high-air landings softer on the rider. Phasers were borrowed from windsurfer and surfboard shapers seeking to create the same loose feel for their designs.

Wakeboarding soon exploded in popularity and continues to do so today. The sport is reported to have grown by as much as 400 per cent in recent years, adding a professional tour and a governing body to help it along the way. One of the reasons is that wakeboarding's top professionals are pushing their sport to new limits on a daily basis. The best have added new elements to wakeboarding that come straight out of skateboarding street style and snowboarding freestyle. These riders are doing grinds off obstacles like channel buoys and docks, and are even jumping on and over rock outcroppings where available.

Tight fit

Wakeboard binding systems have developed rapidly to deal with the added forces riders are putting on their equipment. Initially, the bindings used were simply upgraded or modified waterski-style. The new bindings offer tremendously more support and grip to hold riders on their boards. In fact, the new designs are so snug that liquid soap is generally a standard accessory to aid in getting into or out of the bindings. The reasoning is obvious: create new moves that your equipment can't deal with and you wipe out.

Wakeboarding parks are now being created where once waterskiing parks existed. Wakeboarders are discovering new uses for the overhead pull systems that resemble ski lifts, and now use the added lift to soar up and around the courses, doing spins and other moves never before seen at ski parks. Newer and younger riders are getting into the sport, and it is certain that they will bring with them even more innovative approaches to wakeboarding.

Wakeboarding is poised to do the same thing for waterskiing and tow-behind water sports that snowboarding did to revitalize the ski industry. It also provides a real indication of where board sports are headed... sideways.

Whitewater

Standing on the shore of a raging river is an explosion of visual and auditory sensations. There is a primordial feeling that rushing water sets off in us. To prove your mettle on a raft, canoe, boogieboard, or kayak against the most violent of nature's forces—the fury of moving water—is to participate in one of the most adrenaline-pumping of extreme sports.

THERE ARE VARYING DEGREES of difficulty to consider when choosing which watercraft best suits the needs of the rider. The first and least difficult method of getting down whitewater is via a raft, which can be easily found for hire near any thriving river community. Whitewater rafting is a big business, as it offers the opportunity to enjoy the rush of the ride without most of the risks associated.

Raft or canoe?

Which is not to say whitewater rafting is easy and lacking danger. Reputable tour operators offer quality guidance and top rate equipment, including two of the most important pieces of gear needed, a helmet and a life vest. Any time the river is entered on a watercraft, there are risks, and every year, people are seriously injured or killed on rivers all over the world while on rafts. Having said that, if whitewater is appealing, try a rafting expedition first to see how you like it.

Next in difficulty would be the canoe, which due to the open nature of the design, offers little protection from a capsize. Many canoeists are qualified to run rivers of sizeable power, however, canoes do not offer the "righting" performance (returning the boat to a rightside-up position) necessary in big rapids. Canoes are far less stable than rafts and require tremendous balance skills to ride through areas of whitewater.

The boogieboard, aka riverboard, a device first developed to ride beach surf while lying down, is a new entry into the whitewater-running category. Many whitewater enthusiasts, seeking to push the limits and try a new thrill began riding the foam boards in whitewater with success. One of the pioneers, Bob Carlson, now sells his Carlson Riverboards all over the world, many to top river runners. While certainly easier to stay on top of and right after rolling over, the riverboard is far more extreme than rafting or canoeing. On a riverboard the rider is completely exposed to the elements without

The thrills of whitewater rafting are amongst the most adrenaline-pumping of all extreme sports.

188

the protection of a boat's hull to ward off jagged rocks and absorb some of the shock the rapids can hand out.

The most extreme method of getting down a river, however, is on a kayak. Kayaks offer a completely enclosed hull design that allows the paddler to sit in the opening of the hull and seal themselves in using a neoprene skirt. Because the paddler is able to capsize and right the boat without filling the hull with water, they can handle practically any degree of whitewater. The act of righting a capsized kayak is called an "Eskimo roll," since it was created by the Eskimos. Because of the severely cold water, Eskimos have to stay dry and be able to right themselves without doing what is now called a "wet exit," meaning escaping the capsized boat.

For many reasons, doing a wet exit is the last thing a paddler wants to do unless they absolutely must. First, outside the kayak the paddler is immediately exposed to a multitude of dangers, from massive "hydrolics" (sections of the river where tons of water are being pushed downward), to sharp rocks, submerged logs, and other unknowns. Second, once outside the hull, the paddler's only floatation is their body and their life vest. The drop in floatation makes the possibility of the paddler being driven downward onto a hidden obstacle far greater. More than a few paddlers die each year from

simply getting their foot stuck under a rock, and then being dragged under by the current. These two examples should be enough to illustrate why being able to do an Eskimo roll at will is essential to paddling heavy water.

Kayaks are incredibly maneuverable because of their low buoyancy and highly "rockered" shapes, which vary from design to design. Rocker refers to the curve in the hull from front (bow) to back (stern). The more rocker in the hull, the more maneuverable the kayak. Different designs accommodate different performance characteristics. One example is a slalom kayak. Designed to race through a series of gates, the hull is highly rockered, with sharp, angular projections along the top of the deck that serve to provide greater sideways stability, helping the paddler get across the current to the next gate more easily.

Taking a dive

Another is a low-buoyancy "rodeo"-style, or trick kayak, which is a minimally-buoyant design used in trick contests. The reduced-volume rodeo design allows the paddler to spin the kayak around on its ends effortlessly, as well as performing a number of other tricks. Low-buoyancy kayaks are also the preferred design for high waterfall drops that some of the more radical paddlers enjoy. Waterfall paddling is probably the most

dangerous of all the whitewater activities, depending on the distance of the drop. Small waterfalls of 5–10 feet (1.5–3m) constitute normal conditions in extreme whitewater.

The larger waterfalls that the top extreme paddlers drop into can exceed 50 feet (15m). Clearly the opportunity for disaster exists at these heights, and the paddler must land the kayak end first, either bow or stern. Landing any other way results in "flatting out" (landing hard on the entire surface of the hull) which can severely injure a paddler. This is the kayaking equivalent of a belly flop. If the paddler lands on the end, the kayak dives down into the water with a relatively soft landing. Obviously these types of stunts are reserved for top experts only.

Regardless of the type of watercraft used, there is a system of classifying the level of difficulty for each section of a river. The level of difficulty varies from day to day as the amount of water traveling through a section can radically alter the whitewater characteristics. Rivers are measured in cubic feet, so a river traveling at 3,000 cfs (cubic feet per second) will behave quite differently on a day when it is traveling at 10,000 cfs. Snowmelt or torrential rains can dramatically change a river, and in the case of torrential rain it can

189

If whitewater is appealing, then rafting is the best way of enjoying the rush without most of the risks associated with the sport.

happen instantly. Therefore, it is important that river riders are aware of not only the weather immediately around them, but also the weather conditions upstream.

Learn rivercraft

Rivers are rated on a scale of 1–6. The higher the number, the greater the degree of difficulty. It is important to acknowledge that river sections can vary dramatically in difficulty, and it is not uncommon for a river to change from class 1 to class 6 within a matter of meters. Again, it is vital to get local information on the river before going downstream. The following outlines the classification system:

- CLASS I – easy, occasionally small rapids with few obstacles
    - CLASS II – moderate, small rapids and waves which are easily navigated
    - CLASS III – difficult, rapids, hazards, and irregular waves which should be scouted from shore ahead of time; complex maneuvers will be required CLASS IV—very difficult, long, large rapids and falls with dangerous hazards which must be scouted; precise moves will be required, including rolls; rescues will be difficult
- CLASS V – has extremely difficult, violent rapids and falls with narrow routes and many dangerous hazards; experts only!
- CLASS VI – nearly impossible, routes difficult to identify; only to be attempted by teams of top expert paddlers following all possible precautions.

It's useful to know a few of the terms commonly used in whitewater. *Beam* is the widest part of the boat. *Thwart* is a support which runs across the width of the boat. *Blade* is the thin cross-section, wide profile part of the paddle that passes through the water and provides thrust. *Shaft* is the "handle" of the paddle gripped by the paddler. *Draw* is a paddle stroke 90 degrees to the direction of travel to pull the boat sideways. *J-stroke* is a paddle stroke that ends in a steering maneuver. *River-left* refers the side of the river as it looks to the paddler, while *River-right* speaks for itself.

No one is certain as to exactly when the first boat resembling a canoe or kayak was built, but there is evidence that Polynesian and rain forest cultures used similar water craft. The Eskimos of north America and northeastern Asia are felt to have been the originators of the modern kayak.

Early Eskimo kayaks were built of lightweight wooden frames wrapped in seal or caribou skin. These kayaks held one or two paddlers, and were used primarily for fishing. Early canoes, such as those used by the north American Indians, and later adopted by settlers and trappers, were used for both transportation and hunting

Whitewater raft races are becoming more popular with those addicted to the adrenaline.

Modern recreational canoeing and kayaking got their start after an English barrister named John MacGregor designed a boat he called the "Rob Roy." The boat was based on the Eskimo kayak, and he used the designs between 1845 and 1869 to explore many of the waterways of Europe. He wrote and lectured extensively regarding his explorations.

Purest form of play

MacGregor founded the Royal Canoe Club in 1866, with the Prince of Wales as Commodore, a post he retained until he was crowned king. The New York Canoe Club was founded in 1871 in response to the success of the Royal Canoe Club. These organizations were the first to actively recruit members, and provided a focused agenda for the growth of the sport.

190

Canoes are far less stable than rafts, and require tremendous balancing skills to ride through areas of whitewater.

Kayaking became an Olympic sport in 1936, and remains so today. Twelve of the 16 events are sprints held on flat water. Slalom kayaking is held in whitewater, and requires paddlers to traverse a series of gates, both upcurrent and downcurrent. This event is widely regarded as one of the most physically demanding paddling sports because it requires strength, lightning fast maneuverability skills, and a keen ability to read the currents.

Whitewater as a sport, whether Olympic or for fun, is one of the purest forms of play in a natural and changing environment. It is a great way to get out into the wilderness and enjoy an adrenaline-charged workout, and is one extreme sport that everyone can enjoy at some level.

INDEX